Grief, Growth, & Gratitude

A Journey Back to Love

Caitlin Burr

Copyright © 2021 by Caitlin Burr

www.passionloveandpurpose.com

Instagram: passion.love.purpose

Disclaimer

Cover Design: Dorothea Taylor

Printed in the US

ISBN: 978-0-578-95795-1

Thank You

First and foremost, I want to thank God for getting me through some of my darkest days and bringing me to the light of today. I am thankful He has given me a story to share with others. I am thankful God produced this seed within me and allowed me to share His wisdom by publishing this book. I hope it inspires you to truly heal from your grief and grow into your highest self.

I want to thank all the people who contributed to my journey and growth through different chapters of my life. Your presence made all the difference to help me become the person I am today. I send love to all of you.

Lastly, I want to thank Lesley Burr for being the most amazing mother one could ask for. You are the true definition of a phenomenal mother. I am thankful for the love, support, and happiness you brought to my life, and I will always cherish the memories of this lifetime every day. I pray I am making you proud and becoming the woman you always wanted me to be. Words cannot describe how much you are missed. I love you beyond this Earth.

This book is dedicated to my beautiful mother and the wonderful life she lived. The love between a mother and daughter is **eternal**.

"A Letter to My Mom on My Wedding Day"

By Caitlin Burr

Dear Mom,

The day has come and I'm wearing your dress. I wish
you were here to see me looking my best.

I'm marrying a beautiful man. The man of my
dreams. He tells me he wishes he met the mother of
his queen.

As I walk down the aisle, I know you are already
there. I cannot lie, this is still unfair.

My wedding, the birth of my kids, I need you there.

A quiet whisper then came to me. It was quieter than
a mouse. I heard, *"My daughter, I have the best seat in the
house. I'm an Angel and follow everywhere you go. I'm always
with you and forever don't you know?"*

I walked down the aisle and I was at peace. My
wedding day is now complete.

Love Always,

Caitlin

Table of Contents

Your Purpose

Inspiration is a gift we all hold in our lives. We are meant to inspire and live a meaningful life. Every chapter that has shaped you into who you are today is meant to guide someone else into a better person.

Be kind, be loving, but mostly be an inspiration for someone else. You never know who is watching and who you are impacting on a higher level.

Most people do not like to talk about their pain, which is understandable because it hurts. I was one of these people, but I realized I needed to share a story in hopes of helping others alleviate their pain and be a lighthouse for their path.

We are all searching for something much deeper in life—purpose, inspiration, healing, and most importantly, love. No matter where you are in your journey, there is always something better waiting for you.

I hope this book empowers you to heal, transform, elevate, and love yourself unconditionally.

Preface

Why do bad things happen to good people? I asked this question to myself throughout my life, although I never really understood the depth of the question. Watching the news, you see and hear some of the most horrific things going on in the world and may think, *"I cannot imagine what that person is going through."* You then continue with your day and let the question go until you watch the news again. As I came across my personal traumatic events in life, I asked myself this question again. The question was different this time because I had gained clarity from my own trials. I also learned that the answer to this question might vary based on one's personal experiences of life and the chapter they are in at the time.

Based on this chapter of my life, my answer to the question is simply that traumatic events can open doors for **growth**. When you are in the middle of the storm, everything feels like it is heavy on your shoulders, and you ask yourself, *"How am I going to get through this?"* While you are standing in the storm, you do not realize that you are developing characteristics such as discipline, grace, resilience, and compassion that will benefit your life moving forward. You are probably thinking, *"Why do I have to go through some of* *the most difficult times to gain these characteristics?"* First, if I had not gone through everything, I would not have been able to help others going through similar situations. Second, I would have never believed the amount of discipline, resilience, and compassion I had inside myself the entire time. Most importantly, it helped me start on a new journey of **healing** – specifically **self-love**.

Grief is one of the heaviest feelings that you will ever feel. It feels like a pile of rocks on top of your body that you cannot lift, even if you are the strongest person on this Earth. Grief tends to bring out the shadows of your past because you cannot hold all the emotions inside any longer. Grief is the ultimate test of who you truly are and what you are made out to be.

Growth is necessary to become the best version of yourself. Without grief, there is no growth and no new perspective. Growth occurs every single day, even if we do not recognize it. Grief forces you to grow no matter if you are prepared for it. Growth will assist you in healing wounds that have been hidden for so long. Ultimately, growth gives you a new perspective and an extreme amount of gratitude for the simple things in life.

Gratitude is the core of your soul. It is the bridge

between the past and the future. Gratitude becomes the reflection of the person you look in the mirror and dream to be. It allows you to live in the present, reflect on the past, and look forward to the future. Gratitude is full of love, kindness, and compassion. I am not saying that your journey will be easy, and I am not saying that changes will occur overnight. However, I can guarantee that when you look back on your journey, you will be proud of how far you have come, even on the days it feels like no progress was being made.

This book is not designed to tell you how to cope or provide the answers to your journey. This book is simply designed to bring hope and let you know that you are not alone. We are all connected and relate to one another in some way. I hope my story can be an inspiration to others and show them that grief ultimately leads to growth and the biggest gratitude of your life.

As the book goes on, I promise the content will become lighter. The beginning is heavier to read since it is a clear reality of how dark things once were in my life. I specifically want to share with you how the dark days do not last and how you grow through them to start seeing the light. I want to be open, honest, and hopefully inspire you to grow through whatever situation you are currently facing.

GRIEF

Psalm 34:18, "The Lord is near to the brokenhearted and saves the crushed in Spirit."

Grief, Growth, & Gratitude

Chapter 1

What is Grief?

Before my mom passed, I did not understand what grief was or what it entailed. I thought it was just sad that a loved one died and dealing with the memories. I had dealt with death plenty of times before. My grandparents, cousin, and brother-in-law had died. I was deeply affected by their losses and thought that grief was just that - being affected. I was always told you do not grieve if you do not love; this is a hundred percent true. Well, I loved all of them and felt that I had grieved, but little did I know grief was much bigger than that. I thought you could move on and go back to how life was beforehand. My mom's death was a huge reality check and made me realize the true definition of grief.

Grief is an ongoing journey due to permanent disconnection from someone physically. I will explain further what "permanent disconnection" means later in the book. Grief is an ongoing, uncontrolled rollercoaster with various emotions and a transition in your life that can really overwhelm you. Grief changes who you are physically, mentally, emotionally, and spiritually as well as how you react to everything around you. You cannot tell yourself to stop grieving as it naturally overwhelms you, and you have no control over it. Grief makes you uncomfortable and vulnerable. It constantly reminds you that pain exists. Let me say this, grief looks different for everyone. However, we all can relate to the intense pain behind it. Grief can be a blessing and a deep curse depending on your perspective.

April 2016

Storms come and go in life. In 2016, I felt a powerful storm headed my way. Everything was almost perfect. I was twenty-four years old, just started my career, and was looking forward to moving out of my parents' house within the following year. Life was very promising, but my intuition told me something was about to happen. I guess it is like when you take an exam, think you passed it with flying colors, and before you get the results back, you have a gut feeling you failed then find out you indeed failed. I failed to realize that my intuition was preparing me for one of the most life-changing and traumatic events I have ever experienced.

My mom had been sick for quite some time, and the doctors could not figure out exactly what was wrong. I knew it was not cancer, which made me feel better, and I figured she would get through her illness just as anyone else would. I am not sure why when someone does not have cancer, we tend to ignore other possibilities of a life-threatening illness. My mom was a very private person and protected her family by not telling us how she felt day in and day out. My family and I continued with our routines but could not read between the lines that my mom was dying. I believe we were just all in complete denial.

May 2016

Hurricane Grief was approaching my family at a hundred miles per hour, but we ignored the signs, and there was no safe place to take shelter. My mom's health declined almost overnight. She was in and out of three hospitals within a month, but I continued to ignore my intuition. *"She's going to be alright. She's strong; we will get through this,"* is what I told myself, but I knew something was not right. My mom came home for a week in between the first two hospitals. I remember going to her doctor's appointment and noticed her skin and eyes were very yellow. I thought jaundice just affected babies when they were first born, but at the time, I did not realize it was a critical sign that her liver was failing.

The nurse looked at her with a concerned face and commented on my mom's complexion. I will never forget the look on my mom's face. She was scared. I do not think she was afraid of dying per se but scared of her family finding out that she was leaving soon. She was upset because I wanted to be in the room with the doctor and hear what the doctor had to say about her health. She was trying to keep my family from knowing what was about to happen.

I remember the doctor telling us my mom needed to see a nutritionist. At that point, I knew I had to take charge of her getting on a better diet. After the appointment, I asked my mom what she wanted to eat, and she said, "a slice of pizza and a cannoli from Gianni's," which is a popular pizza place where my family frequently dined. I was so upset my mom asked us to take her to get this food after the doctor said she needed to eat healthier now, so I told her no. If I had listened to my intuition, I would have taken her to the restaurant and given her what she wanted because, after all, it was her dying wish. Even today, I regret not taking her and wish I had given her a large box of pepperoni pizza with ten cannoli's on the side.

My family took my mom home, still hoping something would change, but things only got worse. She could barely walk due to her legs being swollen and full of fluids. She was in so much pain; all she wanted to do was sleep. My family felt **helpless** and did not know what to do except make her feel as comfortable as possible. My dad was a soldier, as he stayed by my mom's side every day for two years, not letting her out of his sight.

One day, I wanted him to have a break. He later went to the store. While he was away, she had to use the bathroom, so I helped her get there. Again, my mom was a strong and private woman who could bury her emotions inside; however, that day, she could not. She was in so much pain; she needed my help. When we both realized I physically could not help her, she burst into tears and told me to call the ambulance. In my twenty-four years of life, I had never seen my mom struggle as much as I did that day. She left to go to the hospital, but I failed to realize that it would be her last time home.

She was at the second hospital, and you know what I did? I did not go to visit her. I know you should not regret things in life, but I absolutely regret not visiting her every day in that hospital. I just asked my dad how she was doing, and that was it. My dad was a lot like my mom; he did not want us to worry, and he kept a lot to himself. He kept it together until that one day when I received a phone call from my older brother.

June 2016

Hurricane Grief had arrived, and it was not going anywhere anytime soon. I remember I was at my ex-boyfriend's house at the time, and my brother told me that my dad had an extremely rough night and that I needed to come home and be with the family. I knew then something was about to happen but still did not accept that death would be the outcome. Your intuition is a blessing in disguise. It warns you about critical things in your life, including things you may love deeply leaving. I came home and heard the good news. My mom was being transferred to Johns Hopkins Hospital in Baltimore, Maryland. It is one of the top hospitals, which gave me hope that my mom was on the road to recovery.

My family went to the hospital, and we sat in the room with my mom and waited for her doctor. Hospitals never really bothered me until this time. I always felt like hospitals gave hope to people who needed to recover, but I never thought a hospital would give me a permanent scar. The doctor came into the room and went right to asking personal questions. The conversation of my mom getting on the transplant list was the best news I had heard all month. After running tests over the next few days, the doctor was eager to get her into surgery and on the path to recovery. My family felt nervous but relieved that my mom was in the hands of some of the best doctors, and she was being cared for. *"Why didn't we think to bring her to Johns Hopkins a long time ago?"* I thought to myself. It felt good going home that night.

The next few days felt like a blur. I was not sleeping well; I was hoping and praying my mom would be alright. I spent long hours in the hospital with her waiting for updates. My family and our friends, who are more like family, came to visit each day. My mom smiled, laughed, and kept the strong fight going in their presence.

I remember one evening we all came into her room, and she told funny stories about her children (as she always did) and in the middle of the story started talking about something else then eventually went back to her original story. A critical sign of liver failure is memory loss; however, I tried to remain positive and enjoy the moment with my mom. At that very moment, I wanted to cry because it really hurt to see the strongest woman I know go through this. She had the brightest spirit in the room yet was in the hospital bed. We all said good night to her and left for the evening.

I always wondered why the eye of the storm was the strongest in the hurricane. I know it is the center, but the hurricane expands so much further. I did not realize that my family was right underneath the eye of the storm, and there was no way out of it, even with the amount of hope we had.

The Saturday before my mom passed is still clear as day in my head. Her memory loss was getting worse; she was agitated and uncomfortable with the pain she was going through, but she was still smiling and laughing. People continued to come to visit her and send well wishes, but the storm was getting stronger. My family and I were exhausted. We had been in the hospital for long hours, barely slept, and were still waiting for good news that my mom was ready for surgery. I was hesitant to leave her that day, but I knew we all needed to go home and take a break. I walked back to the car with my family, then my phone rang. It was my mom. I answered, and she asked me to come back to the room because she needed to talk to me. I had mistaken what she said and thought she meant she wanted to talk to my dad. She corrected me, saying, "*No, I need to talk to you.*" I told her I would be right there, but we all agreed she needed her rest, and we left. Again, I know we should not regret things in life, but I regret not going back to her room and talking to her. Looking back on that day, I believe she wanted to tell me to look after my dad and brothers.

My mom was a special woman who loved my dad unconditionally and was his soulmate. I know she was worried about what would happen to him once she was gone, but the mere fact that I could not hear her say that to me still eats me up even to this day.

I was brand new in my career at the time and was only on my shift for about a month. I felt horrible having to take off from work when I was still new and thought I needed to be working the hardest. I decided that Sunday to wake up early, visit my mom, then go to work. I went to visit her, and it was just us in the room. I thought I would be able to have a one-on-one conversation, but the nurses kept coming in and out of the room. I remember just looking at her, not saying anything. Looking back on that day, I think I was just trying to process how strong she was to go through all of this. My brother had come to visit, and we spent time with her. I never had the chance to bring up what she wanted to talk about. I looked at the clock, and it was time for me to go to work. I kissed my mom and told her I would see her later. That was the last time I saw her awake.

I was exhausted all day at work, but it gave me a little time to get my mind off from everything. Work has always been my outlet, and it was much needed at this time. I came home around 1:30 am, and I could not sleep. I was tossing and turning, and then my phone rang. It was my brother. My heart was beating fast, and I was nervous to answer. I picked up and said, *"Hello?"* My brother told me the doctor had called him and asked him for permission to conduct emergency medical procedures for my mom. Everything he said was a blur. I did not know what he meant by making these decisions, but it made me feel good that he did not say Mom had passed away.

The next day I woke up, I was so excited to go see her. I was planning to meet the rest of my family at the hospital. I finally got to the room she had been in over the course of the week, and she was not there. It was some random man in the room. My heart dropped, and my stomach sank. *"Where was my mom? Why did they move her and not tell us?"* I walked over to the desk, and they told me she was moved to the Intensive Care Unit. Again, I was just so happy that the nurse did not say, *"I'm sorry, your mom has passed away,"* and I rushed up to the ICU, not thinking of what it meant. I have never been to the Adult Intensive Care Unit before, and I did not know what to expect.

I spoke to the nurse at the desk, who told me that only

two people could go in at a time. Also, a full medical suit had to be worn just to visit my mom. I did not care what she was saying because all I wanted to do was visit her. I was told it was okay to go back to her room to see her, and I was smiling so hard because I was so happy. I walked back and froze outside the door. I was at a loss for words and held back every single tear from falling from my eyes. My mom was completely sedated and hooked up to what seemed like one thousand machines. She had a long tube down her throat, and I could not talk to her because she was asleep. I turned around and left to go to the waiting room while holding the tears back. I called my family because they were not there yet. I told them to meet me in the waiting room to not be caught off guard like I was. The rest of the day was a blur to me. I just knew at this point something was going to happen, but I still did not accept death was approaching.

The Tuesday, before my mom passed, was probably one of the hardest days for my family. You know how you must accept the relationship is not working out, but you do not want to because you love the person that much? That is what we had to do with my mom. I was driving to the hospital with my dad and two of my brothers in the car.

My dad received an unexpected phone call from one of the doctors. I remember he had a heartbroken look on his face, but we did not know what was said. He hung up the phone, burst into tears, and said, "*Her organs are shutting down.*" I have probably seen my dad cry maybe once in my life. A strong man who holds his head high was in complete tears, and I felt completely helpless. We got to the hospital and spoke to the doctors, but I cannot even remember what was said. I was completely at a loss for words and still could not comprehend what was happening.

The day before my mom died was extremely emotional for so many people. By this point, a lot of my family, friends, and so many other people were notified that they needed to come to visit my mom. The doctor came into the room and told us she was too sick for surgery, her liver had completely failed, and her other organs were right behind. As a result, she was 100% on life support, and there was nothing they could do. There it was—the moment and words we avoided, the moment we did not want to accept, and the moment that broke us. My family was quiet and took a long pause. Some people cried, some just had a blank face, and some started to ask the doctors questions because they were in denial of what they had just heard. I remember my dad was sitting down, and

I was standing up next to him. He broke down again, and I did not know what to do.

My brother and I continued to call people and inform them of what was going on. I guess that was my way of staying busy and not allowing myself to process what was happening. Everyone said I was so strong and holding it together, but inside, I felt like a shattered glass door—completely broken. So many people came to visit my mom. It was amazing to see the love and support we received. Just about everyone that was able to make it to the hospital did so. My dad just wanted to wait for one last person before taking my mom off life support, my Aunt. She lives in Maine and drove twelve plus hours straight just to come to say goodbye to my mom. The love my mom gave to this world was indescribable. For someone to drive that far in a short amount of time on short notice, it speaks volumes about their character.

June 9th, 2016

The day had come. Everyone who was able to visit my mom did for the last time. In my mind, I thought I was ready and prepared to let my mom go. Let me say this; it does not matter how much you "prepare" yourself and how "ready" you think you are to let go of someone you love, especially a parent, you just will not be. This was the hardest thing I have ever had to do, and it left a deep wound on my heart. I remember a good amount of family showed up that day, and we were trying to get ourselves together mentally. I think a chaplain came into the room and read scriptures to us. I really cannot remember because I just kept staring at my mom. We all said our final "goodbyes" before taking my mom off life support, but it was the most challenging situation ever to go through. We all cried and did not want to let go. I thought to myself; this cannot be happening. It felt like a bad dream you could not wake up from.

So many tears were falling from our eyes, and my family was just completely broken. My mom was the glue that held us together, and we were falling apart in that room. I remember my dad told the doctor he was ready to take her off life support. We all stood close around her. I specifically was holding her left hand the entire time. I can still feel her hand on this day and would do anything to go back to that moment. We all cried our faces out and watched my mom pass away. The official time of her passing was 3:33 pm. Just like that, she was gone! I thought to myself, this cannot be real, and I was in complete shock. Little did I know this was the beginning of **Hurricane Grief,** and it was here to stay.

Chapter 2

Rollercoaster Ride

The top of the rollercoaster always makes my stomach turn upside down. Well, that is how I felt when my mom passed— the same knots in my stomach, with the pause before going down the rollercoaster at eighty miles per hour. I felt like time had slowed down and sped up at the same time. My mom knew she was dying before any of us could process what had happened. She already had flyers of the funeral home she chose weeks prior to her passing away. I did not know at the time, but my brother had found them back in May and literally broke down. My family went to the funeral home of her choosing and sat around a long table. It was one of the most overwhelming feelings to plan a funeral when we could not even process our emotions. The responsibilities involved in planning the funeral were completely ridiculous. I just wanted to curl up in a ball and cry because I thought I should not be going through this at my age. I should be out living my life, not planning a funeral for my mom. However, I tried to stay strong for my family.

I was so thankful that my mom's side of the family was there to support us and help us make critical decisions. I feel like when someone passes away, you are in complete shock; therefore, it should not be your responsibility to make decisions because you will not make the best ones if you have a foggy mind. Our plans were finalized, and we were having the funeral five days after she passed. There was so much to do in a short amount of time while balancing our own emotions. My brothers and I did not want my dad to be more overwhelmed, so we just did everything. I was not sleeping, barely eating, and did not know where to begin with the arrangements.

My dad, two brothers, and I had to see my mom one last time before she was cremated. It was one of the most unreal feelings I had ever felt. My mom was lying in a casket, and this was the last time I was physically going to see her. I think we all were so much in shock that none of us cried that day.

The Viewing

My family decided to cremate my mom prior to the viewing due to the illness taking a toll on her body. I think it was much easier that way because seeing her in a casket would serve as a reminder that she was gone. So many people showed up, and it was appreciated. However, it did not take away the fact that I still did not have a chance to process her death. The love and support seemed to be a good distraction for my family. My brothers and I made collages of her life and put them across the room. Pictures reflected my mom's life from the time she was born up to the time she was gone. All I saw in her pictures were **love**, **happiness**, and a **great life**. The viewing came to an end, and we dreaded the next day—the funeral.

The Funeral

I had been to funerals before, and I thought they were sad, but I had only cried at one. I had been up all-night thinking of what I was going to say for my speech, but nothing seemed perfect. I read what I wrote out over and over to my ex-boyfriend, but it was hard to process what I was writing. I finally tried to sleep, but it was more of a light nap. I woke up and put the dress on. I wore a bright green dress to represent liver disease. Life is funny sometimes because it gives you signs that you do not put together until later in life. My mom always told me that when she passes, she wants us to wear bright colors to her funeral, not be sad, and celebrate her life. I am normally a person that either is always smiling or just has a poker face. I do not cry often, and I do not cry in front of many people. I am just the type to hold myself together until I am by myself somewhere.

I remember it was my brother's and I turn to get on stage and say our speeches. This was not a normal *"Thank you. I won an award"* speech; this was reflection and ultimately our goodbyes. It was my turn to say what I had written, and I could not get past the first line without crying. I had held it together in front of everyone for a month and let it out in what I felt was the "wrong" time, but I got through it because I wanted everyone in the church to know how amazing my mom was. I stood up there and spoke these words:

Some of you may know her as Lesley, Les, or Mrs. Burr, but I know her as Mom. As a kid, my mom always told my brothers and me that we were one of her biggest blessings, but little did she know she was ours. One of my favorite memories of my mom was going to the pool with her when I was about four or five, and she stood in the pool. I would jump, and she would catch me in her arms, and we would repeat this over and over for hours. I am sure she was happy when the lifeguard blew the whistle so she could have a break. Now, when I look back at that memory, I realize that my mom was always there to catch me. Whether it was struggling with writing a paper, taking care of me when I was sick, or simply giving me advice to make the best decisions, she was always there. I will never forget my mother and what she has done for this family, along with all the sacrifices she has taken along the way.

When I was in the academy, no matter how bad she felt, she would help me iron my uniform, have a lunch packed for me, and text me to ask how I was doing throughout the day. On graduation day, I thought to myself I would not have made it through without her. That same day she was not feeling well but still pushed through it all to see me graduate from the academy. Those little things are what molded me into the woman I am today.

Today I wear green in memory of my mother. Liver disease is not commonly talked about and can be a hidden illness. Starting today, my family and I will be raising awareness to highlight the symptoms, causes, and effects of liver disease. We hope and pray that this will help provide cures in the future.

Thank you to everyone, including my friends, neighbors, and my extended family that has shown unconditional love and support during this difficult time in our lives. We are grateful for everything you have done out of your hearts. You have made this trying time a lot easier, and my family is forever grateful.

My mother, Lesley Ellen Burr, was a hero, an amazing mother, and a friend. She will always be in my heart, and her legacy will live on. Today we are celebrating the life of a beautiful woman and the many ways that she has touched all of us individually. Thank you.

I still read that speech from time to time to remind myself that I did one of the hardest things most people cannot do. The services ended, and my family headed back home. The love and support continued to pour into our house. While it was very comforting,

I did not realize that we were just on another incline on the rollercoaster approaching another drop.

Moving Forward

My mom was gone, the services had ended, and now my family waited for everything to go back to "normal." People stopped reaching out as much, cards and flowers slowly stopped coming to the house, and my family was just left to sit and think. This was only the beginning. What people fail to realize is that this is when grief truly **begins**. I sat in my room for three weeks thinking I was fine and that I had been through this before, so I can handle it. What I failed to realize is that my "grief goggles" did not kick in yet because my mind, body, and soul were still in shock. I give a deeper definition of grief goggles later in the book.

I was brand new at my job, and I did not have a lot of leave accumulated, so I decided to return to work after three weeks of one of the most traumatic events in my life. There is no right or wrong answer when to return to your "normal" routine, but looking back, three weeks was way too fast for what I had just been through. I thought that everything would go back to how it was, and I could focus on work again, but I absolutely could not. All I thought about day in and day out was my mom. My dad was a mess and traveled so much that he was gone for weeks at a time. I remember my brother told me he felt up and down, but I did not realize his grief had kicked in long before mine, and I did not understand what he meant at that time. I was trying to make things as normal as possible, but I could not.

The first year after losing someone is the most **challenging**. You go through your "firsts" that remind you the person is no longer here. Her birthday was in July, almost a month after she had passed, but I remember I was in so much shock and was still processing everything. The holidays were approaching, and I knew I wanted to make them as normal as possible for my family.

My mom loved the holidays and went above and beyond to make sure we always enjoyed them. She cooked, decorated, played music, and came up with unique games and activities for us to play. Growing up with my brothers, I do not remember a "bad" holiday because my mom always made sure we had everything and more. For the first holiday, that is what I did: cooked, decorated, played movies and music, and tried to find things that made it seem like she was still here.

The days prior to the holidays were horrible. My dad was struggling with her not being here, and I was trying to be there for him the best way I could. My dad would always say that he is "fine" and everything is "okay," but by me still living at home at that time, I saw the complete opposite. My family got through the actual holidays, which was a huge milestone, but time started to slow down again. I have always not been a big fan of January because I felt like time slowed down and winter was extremely long. This January dragged, and I felt like I had been stuck on a rollercoaster. Time felt like it had stopped, and I was struggling with so many emotions that I felt overwhelmed again. My support system was amazing through the first year, and I was grateful for that. They listened and comforted me the best way they could, even though they could not understand everything I was going through. I felt so **alone** and having someone there can really help you get through some bad days. The months started to become a blur, and I felt like my days ran together. My performance at work was not good. I felt **broken** and like I was walking around in circles. Time seemed to slow down until more major days that deeply connected my family to my mom approached.

Mother's Day

Mother's Day is the hardest day I face every year; it is difficult for me to get through. I walk through the stores seeing a large selection of Mother's Day cards and must accept that I cannot buy one anymore. I avoid getting on social media that day every year because I dislike the fact that I cannot upload current pictures of my mom and me like everyone else. This is the one day of the year that I am envious of those who still have their mothers and can shower them with gifts and love. I also used to get angry at those who ignore or put their mothers down because, from my perspective, at least they have their mothers physically here. I understand we bump heads with our parents in life, but losing my mom made me realize that once they are gone, they are gone. Therefore, you must cherish every moment, even the small stupid arguments, because you will wish you could get all those days back. My family and I spent the first Mother's Day following her passing with my grandmother. It distracted me from thinking that I cannot celebrate this holiday like I used to anymore.

Parent's 36th Anniversary

My parents were married for thirty-five beautiful years. I grew up in a very loving household and was fortunate enough to see two people love each other unconditionally. There was no question that my parents were soulmates and made for each other. I always dreamed of having a marriage with the amount of love my parents had for each other. My dad seemed to be okay on this day, but I still could see in his eyes how much he missed her. Mother's Day for me was probably equivalent to their anniversary.

June 9th, 2017

The one-year anniversary of my mom's passing was approaching very quickly, and I knew that I did not want to be home on that day. My mom was born in Massachusetts, and while her father spent time in the military and she traveled across the world, Massachusetts was a special place to her. My brothers and I spent every summer there with our grandparents; my mom's side of the family still lives there. I suggested that we go to Massachusetts for the anniversary of her passing and spend time with her side of the family. There is no script on how you will feel on the anniversary of the day your loved one passed away. The feeling that explained what I experienced is - weird. I thought after the first year of my mom not being here, things would get better, but that was not the case for me. My mental health was hanging on by a string at times; I was still dealing with grief I tried to avoid, and more hurricanes were coming my way that I was not prepared to deal with.

Chapter 3

Dark Space

I always wondered why bad things happen to good people, especially those who are positive, spread love, and do not ask for anything in return. The grief process is something I do not wish on anyone because it puts you in a space no one can get you out of except yourself. I hated being at work. I did not sleep. I lost a tremendous amount of weight. My family was broken, and I felt so many emotions at once that I did not know how to handle them. You almost feel like you are crazy because the grief is so **overwhelming**.

No one tells you when your loved one passes away how grief will feel (especially since it is different for everyone), but I felt like I should have been warned because I thought something was wrong with me for a long time. I finally looked up what grief is and found the different stages and what it consisted of. The stages I am about to explain are slightly different from the definition, but what I personally experienced. My grief goggles started to kick in, and this is where I entered a dark space.

Denial: She is not really gone, this does not feel real, and this is a mistake are the things I said to myself repeatedly. The house was quieter, the love and joy appeared to be gone, and I could not believe my family just went through this. Denial can put you in a dark space when it comes to grief because you are thinking of every possible way this could have been "different." You start to become obsessed with this stage because you believe there must have been another way to avoid this outcome. I believe denial is one of the strongest emotions you feel up front with grief that sticks around, especially throughout the first year.

Guilt: I felt so guilty about my mom dying. I felt like it was my fault in a sense because *"if I did more, she would still be here."* I replayed so many scenarios in my head over and over, but I continued to feel guilty. This stage can be detrimental to one's mental health after losing their loved one because guilt is the emotion that can drag you down until you sink and hit rock bottom. *I should have done this. If I did this, things would have been different.* I felt responsible for my mom's death and walked around with guilt on my shoulders so much that denial felt good. I spent many nights having nightmares of my mom dying over and over (each time was different), and in the end, there was nothing I could do. These nightmares were horrifying and made me relive my guilt each time, even though it was trying to show me that no matter what I did, the same outcome would occur, whether I wanted it to or not.

Anger: Eventually, denial and guilt brought anger into my life. I was angry with everything and everyone, and it was the easiest emotion to have around me. I heard over and over, "*God does not make mistakes.*" Well, I was so angry I felt that He made a mistake this time. I was not ready for my mom to die. I was not ready to take on the responsibilities I did not ask for, and I was not happy dealing with things surrounding me. I did not have any answers, and I felt like my life was in complete shambles. Why was I taking on the responsibilities of everyone's grief on top of my own? Why did I have to work forty plus hours a week and still come home to deal with others' grief but never get asked about how I felt?

I have always had a big heart, very caring, and very loving, but anger changed me. I felt like no one cared about my feelings or helped me through my trying times. As a result, I stopped caring. I started expressing my true emotions, and people took it as I was just "stressed." Well, yes, I was stressed; that was a no-brainer, but I was also angry and did not care about people's feelings anymore because they did not seem to care about mine. Anger is a stage I continued to work through off and on over the years. It was my best friend at times and my enemy when I was trying to find peace.

Sadness: On the days I could control my anger and be calmer, my new emotion was sadness. I cannot count how many nights I cried, thinking of great memories of my mom or just missing her and wishing she were still here. **It is true that you really do not know what someone is going through, so you should be kind to them.** I was walking around hurting, but it felt like no one could see that or just did not want to deal with it. I had sunken into a deep depression during the first year, and it continued.

I never really understood depression until I lost my mom. I thought it was just a period of sadness that once things started going in your favor, you would overcome. I was wrong about my idea of depression. Depression is like swimming in a pool full of negative emotions, and every time you try to get out of the pool, another negative emotion grabs and pulls you back in. That is exactly how I felt during this stage. I was trying to be positive, move forward, and grow from this. However, depression grabbed hold of me, and I felt like I could not get out. People do not understand that depression brings things that you did not ask for, including insecurities, lower confidence, and a negative mindset that hinders your growth. I fought with the sadness stage of grief a lot, but I counted my blessings each day because I knew this emotion would not last forever.

Acceptance: Acceptance is normally the final stage of grief. The stage everyone looks for right away because you are looking for answers and closures. Honestly, acceptance may be something you will continue to look for because healing takes time as the years go by. **Acceptance can be the most difficult stage in the grief process.** When you learn to accept things for what they are, you can unlock a new level of peace and surrender in your life. When my mom first passed away, I wanted to accept it, but you cannot access this stage until you have experienced the other stages. Acceptance is unique because there is no outline of what that looks like. While I was wearing my grief goggles, I was not going to find acceptance in my mom's death until I was able to pull them off.

What are **'grief goggles'**? Grief goggles are a form of tunnel vision when you lose someone close to you. Everything you think, say, or do connects back to them, and you are lost in your own world because heavy emotions take over. Grief goggles can blind you from the rest of the world and make you feel completely alone. There were times I did not want to get out of bed; I made excuses of why I could not go out with my friends, and honestly, grief was taking over my life. I thought I was handling everything the best way I could, but the bricks on my shoulders were heavy, and the walls surrounding me were getting taller. I finally gave in and decided to go to therapy. I always thought therapy was for the "weak" and that you dealt with your problems internally by burying them inside; however, therapy **saved my life**.

I attended once a week for the first year after my mom passed away, and it was the best decision I had made. The dark space started to get a little lighter. I was slowly working through my grief, and I felt like I was making progress. I had disclosed some personal things, including how I dealt with my problems since I was a child. As mentioned, I thought people should deal with their problems internally. That was my mentality until therapy made me realize that this was an unhealthy coping mechanism. With my mom's death, I realized that I could not continue to hold things internally, especially her death. I was finally able to break open the door where the dark space was. I finally felt like there was a light at the end of the tunnel, and I was pushing forward. However, I did not realize grief has a reset clock that you sometimes have no control over. It felt like every time I made two steps forward, I took four steps backward, starting all over again. It was so frustrating that I was trying, but between grief and my internal self, it was holding me back from what I wanted—**peace**.

Dark spaces can be critical phases in your life because you feel like you are drowning and there is no way out. I had insecurities, low confidence, and doubted myself in every aspect of my life, and it was completely frustrating. I did not want to have any of it, and I did not ask for any of this, so I questioned why I faced these things.

Chapter 4

Is It Over?

I felt like **Hurricane Grief** was starting to ease up on my life. It felt like the eye of the storm had finally passed, and I was starting to "feel better." Hurricanes gain strength when moisture is in the air, and there is warm water on the surface. **Hurricane Grief** had weakened for a little while but circled back around, regaining strength about to hit the Burr family once again.

My Grandmother was 92 years old when grief started to take over again. She was quite healthy, still lived by herself in her Baltimore apartment, and she was still sharp and on her toes about everything. My dad talked to my grandmother every day, and I thought it was great because it kept his mind from my mom for a while. Everything seemed to be getting better, but I knew my grandmother was getting up there in age. I just did not expect things to happen so soon. My Aunt went to see my grandmother one evening and said she did not look well. She took her to the hospital, and her heart rate was extremely low. My grandmother had an infection.

In May 2017, my dad decided it was time for my grandmother to receive full-time care from medical staff. You do not realize it, but as you get older, you become the "parent." Watching your parents get older is difficult to accept, and you want to help them by showing appreciation for all that they have done. My intuition told me to spend more time with my grandmother. I went to see her weekly in the assisted living facility and cherished the small moments and conversations with her. My grandmother was a calm and sweet woman. She loved her family and prayed for all of us all the time. My family celebrated her 93rd birthday, and it was truly a blessing.

December 2017

My grandmother's health declined slowly over the course of seven months. It was different from my mom, whose health had declined in a month. My grandmother became isolated and did not have an interest in the same things as before. I could see it affecting my dad, which was completely understandable, yet also difficult to watch. Losing your wife and then seeing your mom starting to pass away eighteen months apart is not an easy situation to accept, although I could see so much strength in my dad since my mom passed. Two losses in eighteen months were not an easy thing to cope with. Although, I think it was easier to accept my grandmother's passing away because she lived a full, healthy life. While my dad, brothers, and I handled the situation well, my older siblings did not. My grandmother's passing away proved to be difficult for them. My family has been fortunate not to have too many traumatic losses, but unfortunately years later, my nephew was murdered in Baltimore. My family is still trying to heal from this loss.

I know death is a part of life, but I did not understand why I felt I was in a continuous cycle of grief that I could not get out of. I was getting through it but failed to realize that grief was not over for me. I thought grief only occurred when someone passed away. Soon I learned that grief is included when someone is no longer a part of your life, and you must readjust not having them physically around anymore.

Lover Loss

I went through another major loss in my life involving my ex-boyfriend. I had known my ex-boyfriend since I was thirteen years old, and we had dated on and off for a long time. Your first love holds a special place in your heart, and that heartbreak is tough to overcome. Prior to my mom passing away, everything seemed okay between us. He was in the room when my mom passed and was there through some of my toughest days. Things changed, but I could not figure out when they did and why. I made mistakes, and so did he.

Ultimately, things got bad between us when I was in one of the weakest spaces in my life after losing my mom. I was so angry that no matter what I did, it did not seem like it was enough, especially when I was the one who needed a lot of support at the time. I was struggling in my personal and love life. The relationship came to an end, and I was devastated. I was tired of going through so many losses in a short amount of time, but this loss was different. I felt that I was left in a space completely alone and did not understand why.

I went through another cycle of the many phases of grief, especially anger. I lost my mom, my grandmother, and now I had to deal with a breakup. I completely isolated myself from everyone and sunk into a deep depression again. I did not understand why I was suffering so much when all I tried to do was share my love and be the best person I could be.

I never thought I would experience depression in my life, but I was standing in the middle of it. I continued to go to therapy. As I mentioned before, I used to be someone that kept everything inside and brush my problems under the rug, but grief has a way of exploding those bad habits in your face. Eventually, I saw tremendous progress with myself, but I was still hurting so bad. I was sinking into a dark hole that I thought I did not know how to get out of.

Chapter 5

Broken Pieces

Back-to-back losses turned me into a person that I did not even recognize. I was insecure, angry, but most importantly, I was broken. Internal wounds can bring other illnesses such as depression and anxiety, which I fought for an extended amount of time. Internal wounds are not things you can physically see; however, they affect you on all levels - physically, mentally, and emotionally without having an answer for how to "cure" them.

I felt like no one understood what I was going through, and I was completely lost. I was struggling at work, could not find peace, and felt like giving up daily. I repeatedly played music that related to my pain, which made me feel every ounce of what I was going through. Dealing with depression while still having to get up every day to push through was the toughest thing I had ever been through. All I wanted to do was sleep, be isolated from everyone, and stay inside of a bubble. I thought to myself, *"Things are not getting better. I guess this is how life will be for the rest of my life."* I slowly stopped going to therapy and just accepted the cards that were being dealt.

Depression was my worst enemy. Depression is like having a dark cloud over your head that will not leave no matter what you do. The dark cloud feels like it is constantly raining on your head, and the sunny days will never come back. Depression is a lot clearer to see - sleeping a lot and loss of appetite and focus. I had never experienced anything like this in my life, and it really changed who I was. For those who have never dealt with any of these issues, it is not something you can fix overnight.

Grief constantly reminded me of the broken pieces I held inside. I was also constantly reminded of my mom's death. I remember I was at work, and I walked into a hospital for the first time after my mom had passed away. I walked into the emergency room, where people are obviously not in the best shape, and all the thoughts of my mom's final days came back to me instantly. Your wounds can jump right back into what you thought you moved forward from in an instant flash.

Even though I felt broken inside, I continued to have a smile on my face and hid how I felt internally. Most people believed I was still the same person, but that was completely inaccurate. I transitioned into what I found out later in my journey to be a stronger and better version of myself.

GROWTH

2 Peter 3:18, "But grow in the grace and knowledge of our Lord and Savior Jesus Christ. To him be the glory both now and to the day of eternity. Amen."

Chapter 6

Lost Identity

Usually, if something happens to you in your life, you go back to your normal routine when it passes. For the most part, someone who broke their arm will eventually heal and go back to using both arms. Someone who lost their dog will replace it with another one. However, losing my mom, grandmother, and ex-boyfriend was incredibly traumatic for me, and I was still recovering. It is like the rug was pulled from under me three times, and I suffered a concussion each time trying to recover from the prior one. Some people observed that I was not the same person as before. Although I still joked, laughed, and smiled daily, there were so many aspects about myself that were not the same. I later realized that this was the beginning of transforming into a better version of myself; however, it took years for me to see the depth of God's plan for my life.

I became severely isolated from people. It felt like I was walking in the middle of Times Square during rush hour, but I was the only one there. When you endure this amount of pain in a short amount of time, you cannot be as open as you used to be. You become selective of who stays and who goes in your life. Most would say this is a negative factor of growth, but it became the main component for my growth to happen. I turned **inwards** and started to re-evaluate my life.

Who Am I? At that time, I was unsure. I knew who I was once before, but I did not know who I was anymore. Traumatic events change you to the point where you do not recognize yourself. You stand in the mirror and see a reflection, but it is just an empty shadow. I was empty, lost, and did not know this person. I was constantly reminded by people close to me that the pain I felt would not last, but all I felt was pain. Happy moments were short-lived, and the pain came back, sat next to me, and grew deeper into my heart. I was slowly fading into this dark space that no one could save me from. I was drowning in the dark and did not know how to rescue myself.

Anger, desperation, hopelessness, isolation, and emptiness were who I had become. Day in and day out, I felt like life was slowly and painfully passing by. I hated hearing positive things because I felt they would never happen for me. I heard all the comments:

- *"Your mom would not want you to be this way."*

- *"She is still with you."*

- *"Things will get better; this is temporary."*

The list continued, but I brushed these statements off

because things were not happening for me. I struggled a lot in every aspect of my life, but I reminded myself that there was a **bigger purpose** for my life. My dad ultimately was one of the main people I had to keep going for. Seeing him get through these days gave me enough strength to continue to push forward. I want you to know that grief brings emotions from all over, which is normal; however, if you are having very dark and heavy thoughts, I highly suggest going to talk to someone because you have a purpose on this Earth and need to keep going.

I knew I needed to heal, but I did not know how to. I just knew I was tired of grief taking over my life. I knew I was falling into the depths of grief, but I did not want to become stuck in its cycles. I started to look at grief as an opportunity instead of a curse. I said to myself, *"Allow yourself to feel grief, but do not allow it to take over your life. You can allow your situation to spiral out of control, or you can take your* **power** *back and transform your life into something greater from your experiences".* I eventually took all the pain and used it as motivation to become a better version of myself. There is no doubt that all the losses were painful, but I had to remind myself that they were beyond my control, and if I wanted to move forward, I had to eventually allow myself to heal. I later realized that these darker emotions and days were the **foundation** I needed to heal and grow.

Chapter 7

Am I Finally Healing?

I remember one day I woke up feeling happy and at peace for no apparent reason. I looked in the mirror and started to see the beauty in myself versus the dark shadows I saw beforehand. Not only did I start seeing the beauty in myself, but I started seeing the beauty in everything. It was the most calming feeling I had experienced in a while, and I questioned where it randomly came from. I was still isolated from everyone and spent a lot of time working and at home on my days off. I started to realize that being by myself was the peace I was seeking from others. Although several people had been there for me, I had to learn to become my own best friend again. It might sound cliché, but I started "dating" myself in every aspect that I never did before. I went to places by myself, found old hobbies that I used to love to do, and reassured myself on things I was particularly hard on myself for in the past. I started to enjoy being by myself and was not afraid of being alone. Grief turns your world upside down, and it is okay to start new and do things that are beneficial to you. Everybody is different, and for me, I had to rebuild a new version of myself.

I enjoyed being in this space. I then questioned if I could keep this new level of peace in my life consistently. I did a lot of reflection at that time, and

I eventually gained new levels of wisdom. I later realized Hurricane Grief was revealing **deeper pain** inside myself. When my mom passed, I thought I was grieving just her death. As the years went by, I realized I was not only grieving her death but grieving my "old" self. Grief can be related to shedding the unhealthy parts of yourself and transitioning into a better version. Those heavy emotions that I experienced initially were not just from the losses, but they opened the door to **all the emotions and pain I had repressed my entire life**. I was releasing and grieving the old wounds, unhealthy patterns, and the things that were no longer serving me. My pain had an expiration date, and I was determined to leave all this behind. I was ready to start a new healing journey.

I was beginning to transition into a better version of myself; however, I had to **face my wounds**. This energy was not easy to transform at first because I had to understand where all of it was coming from and why. At first, it was uncomfortable unplugging and sitting with myself, figuring out all my deepest pains, the parts I did not like about myself, and facing my past, even though Hurricane Grief had taught me that everything starts with you, including healing. I really dug deep and learned where my wounds and triggers stemmed from. I realized that a lot of my unhealthy habits and wounds stemmed from childhood. An aspect of my 'old' self that I became more aware of on my healing journey was my emotional wound, which stemmed from my childhood. I struggled with this, and it brought a domino effect to how I operated in my life. I learned to bury my emotions, especially the uncomfortable ones, at a young age and not confront things that hurt me, but my mom's passing woke me up out of that cycle. I was very co-dependent on others and wanted to "fix" people. I relied on others to fulfill my needs, specifically my emotional needs, which ultimately is self-abandonment. Co-dependency occurs when you **lose your sense of identity and self-worth through someone else**. You want to be a fixer and save everyone, and you enable their behaviors that ultimately harm you. I was co-dependent my entire life, trying to fix people's wounds and neglected mine. Additionally, I would abandon my needs to fulfill the needs of others. I gave love away freely to the point I was drained. I poured into others but forgot to pour into myself. I would abandon myself believing that was the only way to receive love. Many bad habits stemmed from this, including lack of boundaries, being needy, being manipulative, people-pleasing, looking for external validation, and a lack of self-love. I used to be timid, insecure, and had low-confidence, and did not believe in myself. I soon realized that I was abandoning myself by trying to fix, save, and overextend to help people who were not my responsibility. By doing this, I would lose my identity and self-worth through others. Remember, you cannot fix, save, or control another person. If you are trying to, then you need to reevaluate yourself. At this point, that is what I did. I realized I needed to change. Hurricane Grief taught me that I was not in a healthy space to begin with. I could no longer neglect my feelings, needs, and wants because I needed to put myself as a priority.

As I continued to confront my internal wounds, I discovered more wisdom. I learned that healing occurs **when you want to change**. Also, healing occurs when you recognize that the environment **(which begins with yourself)** is no longer a productive system to operate from when it includes repressed pain and trauma. Healing starts internally. Addressing your internal wounds is how healing occurs; however, you will be tempted to revert to all these aspects because they may be all you know. It can be difficult to identify that we need healing because we may be at a level of denial where we believe there is nothing wrong to begin with, or we fear what it would look like without these wounds. Some signs of inner wounds are pain, unhealthy patterns, fears, insecurities, doubts, negative self-talk, among others. This can come from old beliefs, such as believing you must repress your emotions, or you are not worthy. The biggest challenge for me at first was changing my mindset and environment (myself). I realized that healing takes a lot of 'inner' work, but it is completely worth it. Without grief, I may have not **appreciated the joy** I felt when I overcame this process. When you confront your wounds, you ultimately alleviate old pains and break old habits and beliefs at a core level from recycling in your life. You also may be breaking old generational curses that have been in your ancestral line.

However, the more you heal, the more you will be "tested" to see if you have overcome your "old" self. The key is to remember to be **patient** and allow yourself **grace** if you fall back into parts of your "old" self. This is a huge challenge because, as humans, we want to stay attached to old things because they are familiar to us. It is a gradual process to heal the deeper wounds within you, but it is possible to not operate from them any longer. It is hard to break deep-rooted habits and patterns. I can attest to that. I have been on my healing journey for a few years now and I still revert to my emotional wound sometimes. Healing truly takes time and is more like a spiral than a straight line. When you think you have healed, a deeper layer of healing comes up. The reality is healing is messy, takes time, and can be difficult because it comes in layers. Depending on your trauma and experiences, healing can be a lifelong journey.

I realized that it takes a lot of **courage** to face your pain, trauma, and wounds and become **responsible** for your own healing. Most of our wounds and scars are things we cannot see but hold on to inside. No one else knows the depth of the wounds you carry and cannot heal them for you. Healing is always deeper than what is presented on the surface, and only you can go deeper to identify those internal wounds and where they stem from. Thus, my experiences have taught me that learning deeper levels of yourself takes time. Healing can be uncomfortable; however, to become a healthier 'you,' you must confront the person in the mirror. This process involves a lot of discipline, patience, self-compassion, and self-love. Be gentle through this process because you are elevating into an **unknown area** that you may be afraid of stepping into at first. Healing is not an overnight process and is one of the hardest things to face after being presented with multiple traumas, years of conditioning, and repressed negative memories and emotions.

When you are dedicated to your healing journey, you give yourself a **new beginning**, and most importantly, grow into the best version of yourself. Once we start to see the healing within ourselves, it will begin to reflect on the outside. You will start to lose the 'reality' you once knew when you shed old layers of yourself. You will also begin to observe the world in a different light. As you continue to heal, you will start to observe how many people are unhealed and addicted to trauma and negativity. I was once in that position, but as I continued with this healing journey, I realized that it is okay to evolve away from trauma. I used to relate to others through the similar wounds we carried, but eventually, I realized the more I was healing and elevating away from my wounds, the less I could relate to them anymore. I realized you cannot heal in the same environment that caused your pain. You need to elevate away from it.

Hurricane Grief taught me that before you enter the next chapter of your life, you will need to let go of certain people, old patterns and beliefs, and anything else that is no longer serving you. If people or certain things do not resonate with the next level of yourself (especially a healthier version of yourself) then you may have to leave them behind. It can hurt, but you want to vibrate so high that people and greater experiences meet you there. Of course, it is scary to let go of people, and things you thought were meant to be there forever, but it is more regretful to hold onto these things that you know no longer serve you. You may have to ask yourself, "*Is this person or experience adding value to my life*"? You want to surround yourself with people who match your **vision** of who you want to be in the future. You ultimately want to align yourself with people and experiences that are going to **elevate** you. I learned that you may have to make changes no matter how difficult they may be. We all dream and desire great things in our lives, but to make the manifestations come alive faster, we must make space for new things ahead.

Healing gave me a higher perspective in all aspects of my life. I always questioned the purpose of pain in life. From my own experiences, I have learned that **pain is a messenger telling you something inside of you needs to be healed**. If someone or something triggers you, that is a key indicator that you must go within and find where that trigger stems from. Your thoughts, words, and how you feel are all **messengers** about where you are. If you are experiencing lower feelings, your thoughts are negative, and more than likely, you will also speak negatively. This is an **indicator** that there needs to be some adjustment within you. Of course, pain and low emotions are a part of life, but we have the power to transmute and reduce the severity of it in our lives. No one likes to experience pain, and often we get stuck in it. However, pain can serve as a form of **motivation**. Most people want to distract themselves from feeling their pain, but there may be a hidden gift or strong message behind it. My pain led me to write this book and helped me heal myself on levels I did not think were possible. Pain also became my motivation to heal and grow into a healthier version of myself. You can transform your life and use the pain for something good in this world. You can transform your **grief** into **love** and share your love with others. I also learned that everyone heals differently and in their own time. Thus, my experiences have taught me to be more compassionate and less judgmental of others because I truly do not know what people are feeling inside or the battles they are facing daily.

Hurricane Grief introduced me to **self-love**, and it became a major factor on my healing journey. I decided I wanted to feel good all the time, so I asked myself why not invest in the things that make me feel good and help me ascend. Self-love taught me that pain is temporary and does not always last, even if it is all we feel in that moment. It also taught me to take my power back and be responsible for my own life. Let me say this, self-love is also a lifelong journey and a healthy foundation to have for oneself.

What is self-love? This concept is when you **put yourself first** in all aspects of your life to become a better version of yourself. Many people think it is 'selfish' to put yourself first, but it is the way to attract your deepest desires and live a healthier life. Remember, you must take care of yourself first. You cannot pour from an empty cup. When you make **yourself a priority** in your life, everything will flow. I know everyone's circumstances are different; however, I believe in your journey no matter your circumstances. It is important to learn to love oneself, so you can set the standard on how to be treated by others. Remember, you attract what you are. If you are broken inside and have not dealt with your pain and traumas properly, you ultimately will attract others on that same level. Self-love helped me discover healthier ways to operate from and align myself with who I was becoming.

Self-love will help you discover your true **self-worth**. I discovered mine. I started to truly value myself and acknowledge that I am a special person. This was difficult for me to see at first because I had low self-esteem for so long. I knew I was deserving of so much in life, but until I started to pour love back into myself, I did not realize that I needed to elevate to find it. Your worth is a **rare jewel** waiting for you to discover. After I learned how to love myself on higher levels, I could share more of my wisdom and love with others. You start to see that not everyone will value your self-worth the same way you do and that you hold a special gift within yourself.

With self-love comes **self-awareness**—what you are thinking, saying, eating, and doing with your body all plays a role in your reality. Self-awareness can be extremely beneficial to healing deeper layers to yourself. I became more aware of my thoughts, words, and how I was treating my body, and observing what uplifted or lowered my energy. I must say this is hard work, and you may not want to put this much of an investment into it. However, this aspect of self-love became a driving force in my life. As a result, I replaced old habits with healthier ones. It takes a lot of work, discipline, and consistency, but it is quite possible to turn your life around the way you want it to be.

Self-awareness taught me that when you elevate in your journey and break old habits, it will feel weird at first. It was hard learning how to set boundaries, recognize where I was giving my power away, and let go of the past – to include things and people who no longer served me. It was hard to say "no" when I had always said "yes". Having healthy boundaries and learning to not self-sabotage is important. Self-love helped me take my power back and essentially break most of my habits of co-dependency.

I carried these emotional wounds looking for someone to fulfill them. Instead, I needed to learn how to 'parent' myself and step out of my comfort zone (walking away from being co-dependent and enabling others). I learned I did not have to give away parts of myself to receive love from friendships or relationships. Receiving healthy love can be difficult to identify at first because it looks different without pain and trauma. As I became more self-aware of my habits, I realized that a lot of our pain is connected to our 'inner' child.

Healing Your Inner Child

Hurricane Grief revealed that I was **projecting** all my fears, insecurities, pains, and traumas onto others. I realized that this was connected to my childhood wound. Many of us project our childhood wounds as adults and are unaware of it. I learned that this aspect is so important to heal. Most people are unaware that they are **operating** from their childhood wounds, and eventually it is revealed in relationships and friendships. For example, you may be afraid to leave that relationship you are not happy in because your deepest fear is being alone. This could be associated with being physically abandoned by someone when you were a child. Our pains and fears always reveal deeper things within ourselves. If you have not dealt with things from your childhood, grief will highlight these in a storm for you. Whether it is a breakup, a loss of a loved one, or simply operating from unhealthy patterns. Healing your inner child will free you from the trauma and pain that you have held on to.

How Do You Heal Your Inner Child?

You must identify what your specific wounds are and slowly open them. Let me say that it is difficult to feel that pain—the pain of feeling neglected, abused, abandoned, or rejected from something that occurred in your childhood. However, it may be the leading factor that contributes to your decision making in your present life and holds you back from moving forward. Also, you must allow yourself to **feel** and **face** all the emotions and negative aspects that come with the wounds. It is also important to identify who hurt your "inner child." While it may have been unintentional, you still must find a way to forgive whoever caused you pain so you can heal the wound that you have held onto for so long. You will more than likely repeat cycles if your inner child is left unhealed. There are many different resources to heal your inner child, but you must first address what they are.

Another aspect of self-love is **self-accountability**. I am still learning this one: being self-accountable for your thoughts, words, and actions, identifying the negative attributes of yourself that you do not like, and applying love and discipline to them to change those aspects of yourself. We tend to blame others for our problems and pain, but we also must be accountable. If you start to blame someone else for you not being happy, you must ask yourself, why am I giving them that much power over my own happiness? Instead, look at that individual as a mirror. What do you see in them that is mirrored back towards you? For example, if you believe someone is controlling, you may want to ask yourself where you do not have healthy boundaries set up with that person. If someone is saying hurtful things to you, it may be a sign that you are projecting wounds from within. For example, I was told that I was too needy and had low confidence. While this was hurtful to hear, I later realized that those words reflected the wounds and unhealthy patterns I was projecting onto others. If someone hurts you or vice versa, it reflects what they feel within. Although people may mirror your wounds, that is **not** who you are at a core level.

Self-accountability is difficult. It is difficult to look within and see areas that we need to change in ourselves; however, it can be such an important attribute in our lives. Self-accountability also played a significant role in accomplishing my dreams and goals. At one point, I lacked confidence in my talents, skills, and abilities. I had to be self-accountable and become more assertive to take risks that intimidated me. After I decided to take a leap of faith towards my dreams and goals, I looked back and realized the only person holding me back was myself. It is important to act no matter what the outcome looks like because you never know when your breakthrough will occur. If you fall, you will get back up.

Self-respect was a key component that came about due to all the changes I made in my life. When you show yourself the highest forms of self-love, you step into your power of self-respect.

The key word in this chapter is 'self'. **Healing and transformation can occur when we point the finger at ourselves.** It may be difficult at first, but when we discover our own power then we become more enlightened.

Chapter 8

The Transformation

So, I have talked about the process of healing, but I want to bring further clarification to the **actions** I took to complete a transformation within myself. I focused on the four aspects of our body where healing takes place: physical, mental, emotional, and spiritual. On average, it takes approximately four weeks to implement new habits. However, depending on how deep the trauma and old habits are it may take longer, but do not give up on yourself. I suggest you first write out the areas you would like to confront, heal, and change in all four aspects I listed above. This gives you a visual on where to start in your healing journey, and you can adjust throughout your process. Implementing new habits takes a lot of practice and discipline so keep going even if you do not see results right away. While I was in the process of healing, I embarked on a **spiritual journey**. This led to a new level of healing in my life. As a result, I experienced higher thoughts, more wisdom, and a positive increase in my overall well-being. I discovered several practices that led to a new level of healing and transformation in my life. I also made several changes that enhanced my overall well-being. Everyone is different, and what worked for me may not work for you, but you may be called to do some **soul-searching** when handling a storm that involves grief. I did a lot of soul-searching which revealed the following things that I added to my **daily routine** to elevate my healing and transform my life:

Journaling: I love writing and believe that it has helped me process my thoughts and emotions in a healthy and creative way. Hint: I am writing a book based on my thoughts, experiences, and wisdom. I used to repress all my thoughts and emotions internally to the point that they sat in my subconscious mind, but journaling has become another form of therapy. Sometimes we are carrying so many thoughts that we do not realize that some of them can be transmuted by doing healthy activities such as writing, painting, working out, etc. I journal every day, and it helps me process everything going on in my life and helps me connect with myself. I write down literally everything: my dreams, goals, grocery lists, and ideas. I write down what I am feeling, and I can reflect on my writing later. This has become very soothing for me and helps me not stay in my mind for too long.

Writing positive affirmations has been a driving force in my life as well. "I am" is a **powerful** self-love tool. I mentioned before that I used to have low confidence and was timid. One thing I learned with this process is that words are powerful. How you speak stems from how you think, and ultimately your words create your reality. The key to this is, even if you do not believe your words just yet still say them. I practiced writing and speaking "I am" affirmations for things that did not show up in my life yet. "I am confident" even when I did not feel it yet. "I am strong" even when I felt weak. The key to this transformation process is to stay disciplined and consistent.

Another healthy coping mechanism is to write letters to your past self and future self. You can write about grief and wounds and how you will no longer allow them to take over your life. You can write a letter to your future self about what you would like to see different in your life. **Reflection** is a major key in the healing process. I am not saying you must take this suggestion, but I can attest, when you write letters like this and years later read them, you will deeply reflect on how much you have overcome.

Journaling allowed me to reflect on my progress. I would write down how I felt when I first started this journey. I could see how low I once was. It was interesting to see as time progressed when those shifts occurred within myself. I did not even recognize at one point how quickly I was transforming. Through my writing, I was able to see when the pain started to alleviate.

Meditation: I love meditation and what it has done for my life. It has changed my life tremendously. Meditation brings **many** benefits. It can heal your body, calm your mind, and reduce stress just to name a few. Meditation has allowed me to reduce my anxieties and depression to the point where I feel calm most days. It has also assisted me with healing repressed memories and emotions. This technique focuses on your breathing, sitting in stillness, and reconnecting with yourself. Meditation made me go inwards and observe my thoughts. With this practice, I was able to break old thought patterns and replace them with healthier ones. I was also able to break old conditioning and limiting beliefs I held within myself. For example, I thought being 'wounded' and being 'negative' was normal, but instead, meditation taught me that I could heal and live a healthier and positive life. Meditation also helped me stop living from a fear-based system.

Meditation, in the beginning, was not easy because I had an active and overthinking mind. I felt like my mind would race nonstop, and I could not focus using this practice at first. I started slowly (5 minutes a day), and eventually, I could sit in meditation for longer periods of time, and my mind cleared up beyond what I thought was possible. At times, I even went to sleep listening to meditation music. Meditation made me realize that I am stronger than my thoughts and emotions, and I have power over them. Meditation opened the door to 'reprogram' aspects of myself that were not particularly healthy, specifically old conditioning/patterns.

As I was healing, I had to peel back the layers of old conditioning and patterns. This is extremely difficult because you grow up believing everything that was fed to you. I used to be a negative person, worried about the worse in everything and had an over-active mind. **Meditation** assisted me with breaking old conditioning and led to a more positive mindset and lifestyle. I started thinking, writing, and speaking more positively about myself. I stopped feeling sorry for myself and started changing my narrative. I became someone I once dreamed of becoming.

Meditation helped me shift my perspectives and thinking. Here are some examples:

Through this practice, I was able to change my perspective and ask myself deeper questions. Instead of asking *"why is this happening to me?"* I changed it to *"what is this trying to teach me?"*. I asked myself *"why do I think this way"* and challenged my old mindset and beliefs. The answers were then revealed to me.

I learned that what I thought of myself was more important than people's perception of me. The opinions of others stem from their own experiences, traumas, insecurities, etc. I stopped being a perfectionist, validated myself from within, and stood in my own identity of who I was becoming. Everything I was looking for in another person, I had developed within myself first. I stopped comparing my journey to others because I realized that my journey is unique to me.

I started believing in myself more and shining the light for others to believe in themselves as well. I challenged what society's beliefs were and noticed that those beliefs might not fit with the narrative I was trying to write for my life. For example, many people portray success by what you have externally (big house, nice car, jewelry, etc.), but you can still feel empty inside. I learned that how you feel internally is just as important as what we portray on the outside. Those possessions are just temporary. I used to think of materialistic things, and anything that gave me instant gratification was fulfilling. I later realized those external things only covered up what I was dealing with internally. Of course, having material items are nice, but my well-being became my number one priority.

What is more meaningful is overcoming the battles that you deal with every day in your mind. Success shows up when you learn to genuinely love yourself unconditionally and overcome your past that has weighed you down for far too long. When you observe progress within yourself, you have found true success. The gifts and characteristics you gain leave an eternal impact on others and a long-lived legacy on this Earth.

Another pattern/old condition I transformed was the 'lack mindset.' I stopped focusing on what was missing in my life and started focusing on what I already have. This was a powerful change because the lack mindset took away from the gratitude and abundance that was already in my life. The lack mindset stems from a fear mentality and voids we hold within ourselves. As I broke this pattern/old condition, I learned that the **present moment** is where your happiness and healing start. The present moment is the only thing that exists. The past is the past; you cannot change that. The future has not arrived yet, but the present moment is promising.

Through meditation, I gravitated towards more spiritual techniques and energy practices to help me heal myself, such as healing my chakras. Chakras are seven energetic areas within our bodies. They include the following: crown, third eye, throat, heart, solar plexus, sacral, and root chakras. Each chakra has a specific meaning and is connected to a portion of our bodies. Yoga and meditation are two practices that can assist with this technique. A brief way to explain chakra healing is with this practice; you are finding an inner balance within yourself. If you need more clarification, I suggest that you do your research to gain more information.

A key component that I learned about my chakras was the importance of grounding myself **daily**. Grounding also brings many benefits such as reducing anxiety and stress. When you are grounded, you feel centered and balanced within yourself. This technique helps you reconnect with yourself and brings you back to the present moment. There are **many ways** to ground yourself and this technique looks different for everyone. Think of an activity where you are not overwhelmed, and you feel balanced. It could be yoga, gardening, or going for a daily walk. For me, it is writing. You can also ground yourself by spending a lot of time in nature. It can heal your body and allow you to let go of the old energy you are holding on to. Many refer to this as 'earthing'. Grounding also focuses on releasing old energy in exchange for attaining new energy. You are connecting with the Earth to rebalance yourself. For this concept, think of it as your desire for a new dining room table in your home. If you do not get rid of the old one, then you may not have space for the new one to come. It is important to **consistently** ground yourself in a world full of distractions, disruptions, and chaos. Life can be busy, and we can become ungrounded or unbalanced. When I become ungrounded, I start over with the basics of self-love until I am back on my path. I unplug from social media, spend a lot of time in nature, write, and meditate. Once I feel rebalanced, I can move forward. Remember, you can never go wrong with self-love because it will always bring you back to your baseline. It is also important to have a self-love routine even if you have five minutes to yourself each day because it can keep you balanced.

Another way I renew my energy is by saging my home. This technique allows you to cleanse your energy and clear any negative energy that you may have absorbed. Saging refreshes your energy.

These practices have had a profound impact on my

healing journey. **As a result, I rarely battle with anxiety and depression anymore.** Spirituality has deeper aspects. There are more practices that can help you heal and stay balanced. If you need more clarification, I suggest that you do your research to determine the practices that are best suited for you.

Changing My Diet: Self-love taught me that everything I was feeding into my body (food, what I watched, what I read, what I listened to, etc.) mattered. I used to eat processed foods and fast food all the time. As I started my self-love/healing journey, I realized that I needed to change my diet. I learned that food is medicine and can heal the body. I started meal-prepping, which was a lifesaver for me. I became conscious of the ingredients in foods, replaced them with fresh foods, and even eliminated certain things I used to eat. When I eat out now, I am more conscious of what I order, and I observe how my body feels after I eat. If the food increases my energy, I know that my body has accepted it, but if I do not feel good afterwards, I know that I cannot eat that food anymore. Additionally, I stopped drinking alcohol and increased my water intake tremendously. I noticed that my mind was a lot clearer than ever before in my life.

Changing my diet also led me to use natural products for other normal routines (toothpaste, hair products, feminine products, skin care, etc.). Once I incorporated these changes, my body did not respond well when I tried to revert to less natural products. I learned that it will take time for your body to adjust to the changes, but eventually you will feel a significant positive difference.

Exercising: I have always been into physical activity of some sort, but after my breakup, getting back into exercise became therapy for me. I got back into the best shape of my life, and then I realized that I just enjoyed exercise because of how it made me feel. At first, I was committed to weightlifting, but now I do any type of exercise that makes me feel good.

All the changes I incorporated made me more aligned with listening to my body, which is so important. I was able to identify when my body needed rest, when it needed the proper nutrition, and when it needed to exercise appropriately. My body would tell me when it accepted something and when it rejected it. When I began to elevate, it was easier to identify with things that uplifted me and those things that brought me down.

Practicing Gratitude: This is one of the most

powerful tools I used. I started speaking and writing every small thing I was grateful for. For example, I would write things down like "I am thankful to enjoy a nice sunny day" or "I am thankful to have good health." I know that this may seem tedious, but I added this to my daily life, which made me thankful for everything around me.

As I started writing and speaking of my gratitude for everything in my life, I was able to change my mindset into an **extremely positive one**. I was able to also look at life from a different perspective. I used to complain a lot, but then I realized the more gratitude I practiced, I could see how much I was already truly blessed in life. I started appreciating what I had on all levels and enjoying the present moment more.

Inner Voice/Intuition: Now, this tool is something we all have inside of us. This is a gift to us all and is an important component in transforming your life. Through meditation, I was able to reconnect with my inner voice and intuition on a deeper level. At a young age, most of us are taught to lean on external validation and look for answers outside of ourselves. One of the most important things I learned in my self-love/healing journey is to listen to my inner voice. Your inner voice will not steer you wrong and is a treasured asset. I learned that you have everything you need inside of you and do not need to seek anything. You more so should want to attract what you desire. The key to hearing your inner voice/intuition is sitting in a place of stillness. This takes a lot of practice, but it is important to be in a place of stillness so you can disconnect from outside noise and distractions. Stillness is important because you can miss the answers and clarity you have been seeking if your environment is too busy. As you listen to your intuition and inner voice more, it will strengthen. Another person cannot wholeheartedly give you the advice you seek because they do not live your life. They do not see your visions the way that you do, they do not have the same trials that you may come across, and most importantly, they may tell you what is best for you through their eyes. Your intuition is the guiding light within yourself. You will learn how to be open with others without giving up what your intuition tells you. Sometimes it may be difficult to accept the answers our intuition is telling us, but there is always a greater purpose for what answers you are receiving internally.

From these practices and changes, I have gained a consistent daily practice for myself. For example, when I get up in the morning I pray, meditate, and ground myself even if it is for five minutes. This helps me stay in the present moment and renew my energy every day. Eventually you will transition into a new lifestyle for yourself and observe positive changes within your daily routine. **It is important to pour the energy into yourself first before going out into the world and using your energy there.**

I enjoyed making these changes within myself and I continued to discover other aspects that expanded my transformation.

Chapter 9

The Transformation Part II

Sometimes when we go through a series of grief, we forget old hobbies that we used to enjoy doing that could go back as far as childhood. For me, it was reading. I stopped reading over the years, but through this journey, I was able to rediscover it.

I read books that helped me with healing, enhanced my life, and supported the direction I was going in. Reading helped me connect to other people who were going through the same experiences and helped me understand things I did not process just yet.

Here is a list of books I read to assist in my healing journey:

- "Letters From Motherless Daughters" – Hope Edelman

- "Healing After the Loss of Your Mother" by Elaine Mallon

- "Jump: Take the Leap of Faith to Achieve Your Life of Abundance" by Steve Harvey

- "Good Vibes, Good Life: How Self-Love is the Key to Unlocking Your Greatness" by Vex King

- "Let Love Have the Last Word" by

Common

- "The Power of Now" by Eckhart Tolle

- "Empty Out the Negative" by Joel Osteen

- "The Wait" by Devon Franklin and Meagan Good

- "The Seven Spiritual Laws of Success: A Practical Guide to The Fulfillment of Your Dreams" by Deepak Chopra

- "The Laws of Lifetime Growth: Always Make Your Future Bigger Than Your Past" by Dan Sullivan and Catherine Nomura

- "Battlefield of the Mind: Winning the Battle in Your Mind" by Joyce Meyer

- "Relationship Goals" by Michael Todd

- "Theory of Happiness: How to Find Your Purpose and Be More Joyful" by Dominick Albano

- "Winning the War in Your Mind: Change Your Thinking, Change Your Life" by Craig Groeschel

I also surrounded myself with positive messages and words in my home. All these aspects contributed to reducing negativity in my life. I realized that what you focus on will grow. If you are negative, that is what will be reflected to you. If you are positive, more of it will show up.

Music: Listening to music was a key component in my self-love journey and healing process. Music really got me through some of my toughest days and kept me uplifted on my better days. This may be something so small, but it brought a lot of healing to my life.

Dreams and Goals: I put all my energy and focus into my goals and things that made me happy. I was so focused on myself and accomplished so much in a short amount of time. This contributed into my healing journey because it made me feel good inside when I accomplished personal goals. However, happiness does not have to solely stem from an external item (job, relationship, etc.); it can simply come from within. For example, when I started observing my growth in the healing process, it simply made me happy to see how far I had come. When I changed unhealthy patterns, I acknowledged that I achieved a personal goal. That gave me more energy to continue the process without putting any pressure on myself.

I learned that when you put all your energy and focus into your dreams and goals they can manifest at a rapid pace. The key is to identify what is distracting you from achieving them and adjust accordingly. I must admit this is one of the most difficult changes to make because some things you give your energy to, you may not believe, are distractions. Today, I limit my time on social media and rarely watch the news anymore. It has also given me a new profound peace in my life. I started to realize that a lot of these distractions were contributing to negativity in my life.

I also wrote the personal goals I wanted to manifest onto sticky notes and the steps needed to achieve them. I placed them on my wall and then adjusted my routine to work towards them. I also made a vision board of what I wanted to manifest into my reality. This drew a picture of what I wanted to accomplish. Once I eliminated distractions, I manifested my dreams faster than I had imagined.

Applying the 5 Love Languages Towards Myself: Words of affirmation, Acts of Service, Gift Giving, Physical Touch, and Quality Time. Many people question how they can apply the five love languages to themselves, and it can be quite simple. Everything you are looking to another person to fulfill for you, you can do it first for yourself. Here are some examples of things I did for myself:

Words of Affirmation: Create a positive affirmation jar. For a year straight, I wrote down one positive moment or one thankful moment, or an accomplishment I had each day. This not only strengthened my relationship with myself, but it increased my gratitude scale, including the little things to be thankful for in my life. Another thing I did was download an affirmation app onto my phone. On the days I felt lower, these reminders reminded me of the great things I hold within myself, and I was able to lift my spirits. It is also essential to speak to yourself in a gentle way. This is extremely important for your journey. I was hard on myself and criticized myself every time I believed I messed up on something. Using this love language, I was even more gentle with myself and worked on validating my own decisions. I would also tell myself, *"I love you unconditionally"*. It is important to tell ourselves this just as much as we tell others.

Acts of Service: I did things for myself (even some responsibilities I did not enjoy as much). I made myself enjoyable meals, including meal prepping each week for work. I got all my chores done before the last day of my weekend so I could enjoy my last day off. I ensured that I was helping myself to help things flow a lot better daily.

Gift Giving: I treated myself to things, especially when I reached an accomplishment in my life. Some gifts were more costly (depending on the size of the accomplishment), while other gifts were small. Now you do not have to go on a shopping spree for this language. Sometimes, it could be something as small as buying flowers for yourself, if you like flowers, and enjoy adding them to your home. At times, I bought gifts that would enhance my lifestyle of healing. For example, I bought a nice blender because it enhanced my lifestyle of eating healthier in my daily life.

Physical Touch: You are probably wondering how you can use physical touch towards yourself, but this one is easy. Every now and then, I treated myself to a massage. I did a facial skin care routine every morning and night. I made sure to stretch my body and have a consistent exercise routine to take care of my body.

Quality Time: This love language can be tough for a lot of people, including myself. Earlier, I mentioned that you must unplug from the distractions to begin to heal. I started to check in with myself, asking myself how I feel and went even deeper with asking why. I started meditating, and this was an essential tool to rest my mind. Many people do not realize that their minds are too busy with thinking, distractions, and ultimately are too noisy. As I mentioned, at first, meditation was difficult for me because my mind was busy, and I had to learn how to quiet it. I was able to learn how to connect with myself and understand how I was feeling and where these emotions may stem from. Quality time really helps you get to know yourself and understand deeper parts of yourself you would not think about on a normal day. You learn your deepest desires, what your triggers are, and even discover childhood wounds you never healed from.

Outside of practicing the five love languages on myself, I was able to inherit some great characteristics that added to my self-love journey, such as **patience**. The emotions of grief are unpredictable regardless of how many years go by after you have experienced loss in your life. While I made tremendous progress with moving forward after my mom passed away, I still had moments of sadness, anger, and a hard time with acceptance. Even though patience reminded me that it is okay not to have it together all the time and allow grace to come in, I am still learning every day how to cope with grief.

Another characteristic I inherited was **forgiveness**. This is also a major characteristic to have during the grief process. I had to learn to forgive myself after losing my mom and my ex-boyfriend. It is common to have those thoughts like *"Did I do enough?* or *If I did this, they would still be here,* or *What did I do wrong?"* Forgiveness is an essential component of your healing process. It is not only essential to forgive yourself, but others as well. Without forgiveness, you may delay your healing. Ask yourself, *"who do I need to forgive today?".* It may be your parents, an ex, or **more importantly yourself**. I had to remind myself of one simple thing. Sometimes in life, things are out of our control, and we make mistakes along the way, but with forgiveness, we can move past it and start a new beginning within ourselves for a better future. Forgiveness allows you to release all the pain, trauma, and things that no longer serve your highest good. It brings in a new profound sense of peace and really sets you free.

One way I practiced forgiveness was by saying the Hawaiian mantra out loud. I would acknowledge the person I was forgiving and repeat the mantra as many times as needed until I felt lighter. This helped me to forgive the person and let go. This mantra can be used towards yourself as well.

"Caitlin, I'm sorry. Please forgive me. Thank you. I love you".

While it is great to give yourself a timeline on your healing journey, it is also important not to put too much pressure if you do not reach your goal in 'your' specified timeframe. It is essential to remember that healing is a difficult process, especially if you are dedicated to moving forward. You are changing your behaviors and patterns and setting boundaries for yourself that you may have lacked before. I know this is still a challenge for me, but it truly helps with self-transformation. Remember, tomorrow is not promised, and we must choose how we want to live our lives. Do we want to hold onto pain that may hinder our growth, or do we want to be at peace and flourish into our higher selves? It can be difficult to decide at first, but if you put yourself first, it will become clearer to you what the best choice is for your well-being.

When you begin to heal, you become a magnet for people who are on the same wavelength as you and sometimes assist you with your journey. One day, after having a rough night working at my part-time job, a woman that I briefly spoke to in the past unexpectedly came up to me and told me that something told her to come over and talk to me because I looked like I needed some encouraging words. It is funny how people can feel your energy, and the most kind-hearted people know when you need some uplifting in your life. I remember that day clear as can be because it reminded me that the most precious things in life are free. A smile, laughter, and encouraging words are some of the most fulfilling gifts we can give ourselves and others, yet we sometimes overlook those things.

The best thing I could have ever done is invest time and love into myself, which ultimately created the biggest transformation in my life. I look at my old behaviors, patterns, trauma, and pain as a blessing in disguise. My emotional wound, specifically my co-dependent habits, showed me where I was blocking myself from receiving true divine love within. It also highlighted where I needed to build my own stability and security, which is my own happiness and identity. I realized that success is when I find my own emotional fulfillment instead of relying on others to fill that void within me.

I overcame suicidal thoughts and heartbreak. I beat anxiety and depression. I turned all my weaknesses into my strengths. I transmuted my repressed emotions and memories into higher thoughts and broke old habits. Remember this; you **can** take the bad of a situation and turn it into a new beginning. You can take those lessons turn them into wisdom and apply them to the next chapter of your life. You can heal and be free from dead-end situations. You can literally do anything you put your mind to; you just must first **believe** in it. Grief taught me all these lessons so I could see this more clearly.

Healing is one of the most **rewarding gifts** you can give to yourself. You can have a clear mind; you can break unhealthy behaviors and patterns and let go of unhealthy relationships. You will be proud to see all your progress and be able to create a new version of yourself. You will get to witness your growth and cherish every incident that has shaped you into the person you are today. You can create the life you have always dreamed of for yourself. Healing is not only a gift to yourself, but it brings other great aspects that are more rewarding, including your personal peace.

Chapter 10

Protecting Your Peace

For the past twenty-nine years of my life, I have always helped others not because I felt like I needed to, but because it is a part of who I am. Before my transformation, I was searching for peace in other people except myself. I learned that your peace, happiness, and anything else you seek from others must come from you first. Protecting these aspects is so important because it is easy to forget about yourself in the middle of life.

When you show yourself true self-love, anything trying to interrupt your peace will be highlighted, and you will be able to adjust accordingly. Remember, you are already **whole**, and anything external should add **value** to your life, not subtract from your foundation. At first, it was difficult adjusting to living a peaceful life. I was used to living with unhealthy patterns, an over-active mind, and associated myself with drama. As I healed, I discovered what true inner peace felt like. I then realized that I did not have to live from a place of constant chaos.

Think of a time that you were extremely stressed out. Then, imagine when you go to the beach, and you hear the ocean. The waves are so soothing and make you forget about your stress. Well, when I healed that is what I felt all the time internally. I realized I made tremendous progress after battling anxiety and depression for years. This became my normal foundation, which I valued and enjoyed. Of course, I still get unbalanced; however, it is easier to recognize, and I adjust accordingly. Once I had a glimpse of my true inner peace, I made sure to listen to my soul, so I could keep it close by. Protecting your peace is also so important because you can truly find the **answers** you have been seeking your whole life inside of you. **Remember, we all have divine strength and wisdom within us.** When you are at a peaceful place, you can gain clarity and wisdom that you never had before, but most importantly, you can obtain the happiness and freedom that your heart has always desired.

Hurricane Grief provided me the opportunity to create this foundation within myself; however, this was not an overnight process. I took everything I learned over the years and prepared for a better chapter. Initially, it was difficult to identify who and what were not adding to my peace. As time passed, it became easier to identify what was not aligned with my foundation. How do you identify if someone or something is taking away from your peace? First, you must identify your normal baseline when you are at peace. Personally, I feel a sense of calmness and stillness within myself. I feel like I am in a meditative state (my mind is relaxed), but I am not actively meditating. Some signs that you are not at peace are feeling drained (especially if you are drained for a long period of time), you are constantly thinking of your problems, and your circumstances are harming you. Remember, you do not have to apologize for anything that does not align with your personal peace. As you heal, you will not recognize yourself, as you will be transforming into the new person you are creating. A better, more peaceful, and healthier version of yourself is pure growth.

Once you gain this aspect of yourself, anything that does not resonate with you anymore will be easier to identify including holding on to old energy and pain. **At some point, you must let go of your past.** Sure, it hurts! It also alters how you make decisions and deal with things. I would be lying to you if I said that the trauma did not limit my possibilities out of fear of being hurt again. I held onto my past and trauma for far too long, and it delayed my growth at certain points. However, if you decide not to confront and heal the old pain, you may be on a continuous journey searching for peace. Therefore, you must drop the baggage that is weighing you down. It affects your well-being and, most importantly, takes away from your personal peace. Remember, it takes courage to forgive and let go. If you do not release resentments and anger, it only harms you in the end.

I was in a space for months where I felt calmer than I ever felt and reminded myself that everything would be okay. I was in a peaceful place and wanted to continue to heal. I owed it to myself to be the best version of myself and be happy again. I was focusing on myself but had to revisit some of the traumatic events that hurt me in my past to truly heal and move forward.

My ex-boyfriend, after five months, reached out to me. Five months may seem like a short amount of time to some, but it was a long five months for me to reflect, learn, and grow. Within that timeframe, I had gained so much wisdom from this relationship. I made mistakes; he made mistakes, but ultimately, I learned to forgive him and, more importantly, myself.

Earlier, I mentioned the phrase "permanently disconnecting" as associated with grief. My ex-boyfriend was a product of me permanently disconnecting from him. Grief is not just associated with someone dying; it is also like losing someone that is still here but removing them from your life.

You still feel the effects of grief even in a breakup and after that person is gone.

I concluded that my peace was one of the most valuable gifts at this point in my life. I learned that it is possible to love people even if they are not physically around anymore. You love them for the chapter they were a part of in your life, the lessons that they taught you, and ultimately showing you where you need to grow within yourself. That is a product of my healing and protecting my peace.

Whatever you are going through, whether it is a loss of a family member, relationship, or friendship, I encourage you to allow yourself to address the emotions (good and bad), reflect, and simply find the love within to forgive. When you do this, you will create peace within yourself. You owe it to yourself to identify your grief and not let it overwhelm your life any longer.

You can rewrite a new chapter at any time in your life. As I healed, I decided to build a foundation that revolved around my personal peace. It was rewarding for me, and I learned that you can be a guiding light for others. We are all here to love and help one another, including ourselves. People will recognize when you are in a better space, and you can be the light to show them that it is possible to overcome traumatic experiences and live a peaceful life. When you overcome the storm and create healthier ways for yourself, you will reflect on the deep gratitude you have for your journey.

GRATITUDE

Psalm 28:7 "The Lord is my strength and my shield; in him my heart trusts, and I am helped; my heart exults, and with my song, I give thanks to him."

Chapter 11

The Gift of Gratitude

At one time, I disliked Hurricane Grief. I thought the storm was destroying my life and I was going to sit in the darkness forever. However, I later realized Hurricane Grief just initiated the wounds I had been carrying, and when my mom passed away, I had to confront everything. Ultimately, the storm came to help clean up my life. Hurricane Grief showed me where I needed deep healing and it was a constant reminder that when I thought I was "done" healing, that I still had more work to do. Sometimes, the storms we believe are "destroying" our lives are the things God or the higher source you believe in wants us to reevaluate. For me, this hurricane came into my life at the right time because I needed to reevaluate who I was, how I was living my life, and where God needed me to grow.

There is purpose behind your pain. It may be difficult to understand what that purpose is when you are in the middle of a storm; however, clarity will always find you. It is then your free will to accept or deny that clarity. From my experiences, trauma and pain became my greatest motivators to transform my life.

Hurricane Grief introduced me to growth, healthier ways of living, and gave me the biggest gift of my life:

gratitude. Hurricane Grief enhanced my gratitude for my mom. My appreciation for her continues to grow. My mom will always be my source of strength and light in this life and the one after it. While I never thought I would lose my mom when I did, it happened, and I am continuously learning how to live life without her. I am forever grateful for having Lesley Burr as my mother. In my eyes, she was the most loving and caring mother out there. Her love runs so deep that I can still feel it today, and I will always cherish everything she did for my family and me.

I am thankful for growing through the storm. I gained many gifts within myself that I can use moving forward in my life. I also hold deep gratitude for my life due to overcoming life's hardships and everything I have learned along the way. Going through the darker days made me appreciate the light which is every day in my present moment. When you have experienced the lowest point of your life, you find a deep gratitude overcoming where you once were.

I am thankful that Hurricane Grief shifted my perspective of each chapter in my life. I use each moment as an opportunity to become a better version of myself. For example, I am thankful for the period of being single in my life. It has been so healing for me and allowed me the opportunity to completely focus on my healing and get to know myself on deeper levels.

I practiced gratitude daily for every small thing for years. This eventually became my normal baseline of how I perceived everything. I now hold gratitude even for all the lessons I obtained during my journey. It also opened the door for more positive experiences to come into my life. I try to speak, think, and be positive because life is too short to always be negative and complaining. It increased my overall well-being and my faith. I have grown to have a deeper appreciation of the small things, which gives me a deeper meaning to life.

Everything I went through made me realize that even when I have ups and downs, I can always find the light within to bring myself back to a place of gratitude. Sometimes, you must give yourself more credit for the things that you have already overcome. When you have gone through traumatic experiences and overcome them, you know that you can overcome anything. This thought process brings me back to a place of deep gratitude on my journey. Grief is not an easy thing to confront, but it also gives you the fuel to light your own fire. It brings out the strength and courage we may not have known existed until the storm came to interrupt our lives. Again, our experiences can provide hope, love, and healing to others in similar situations.

How do you bring yourself back to a place of gratitude on your lower days?

I reflect on the wisdom I have gained from my journey. Sometimes, life can be so unpredictable and throw things that you do not expect, but we can take our experiences and use them for something greater.

I wanted to give up so many times when my mom passed because I felt that I did not have enough strength and courage to keep moving forward. We are **powerful beings**, and while grief can feel overbearing and seem impossible to overcome, the light inside of us will always shine through.

Remember, grief and everything you feel with it is naturally normal; **the heavier emotions will pass.** If you revisit some old wounds and pains from grief, remember that is also perfectly normal. You cannot hold an expectation of yourself to be a hundred percent all the time. Give yourself the space, time, and grace to grow. Here are some key reminders for you on your lower days:

1. Love yourself unconditionally.

2. Sometimes, the hurricanes come to build a stronger version of yourself.

3. Take care of yourself and accept the many resources available to you. Reminder: it is okay to ask for help, and you do not have to do it all on your own.

4. How you feel today with grief will pass. You must believe in your process and your growth.

5. Most importantly, keep your faith in whatever you believe in because it saved me. Remember, faith is meant to expand and grow while you are growing through storms.

Living with grief is a critical time in your life that takes a lot of deep reflection on how to move forward. You may be completely lost to who you are and where you are headed. It can be a time of so much change and growth that you look in the mirror and may be a new person every day. You are constantly changing, which is okay.

Life is a journey, including the highs and lows.

Hurricane Grief turned my world upside down, but I am **living proof** that you can really transform your life the way you dream it to be. We all experience grief at some point in our lives, but brighter days are always ahead.

Move forward with gratitude for every moment in your life. Let go, surrender, trust, and take those leaps of faith. I am not saying to drop your boundaries and abandon yourself, but let your gratitude be bigger than your pain and fears. Allow them to alleviate so you can move forward in your life. You do not have to be a prisoner to grief any longer.

Chapter 12

Dear Grief, Thank You

Dear Grief,

Without your storm I would have never learned to face my wounds. Your darkness showed me where the light has always been – inside of me. You gave me the motivation and determination to heal not from only my mom passing away but from everything else I was hurting from in my life. I used to believe that once you experienced pain, you had to live with it. I had an attitude of *'that is just life.'* You showed me where I have been holding onto pain and I was keeping myself inside a box. You gave me the **courage** to heal my heart. Although, I cannot lie. It was challenging because I had to address the pains multiple times before I was at a better place within myself. You taught me that life is supposed to be lived freely with deep gratitude and love, even when we go through those dark chapters.

You reminded me that pain will alleviate, and my love is more powerful and stronger than any storm that comes my way. I became more open to receiving love, wisdom, peace, and happiness. You showed me that my heart is a sacred space I hold within myself. I started to flourish in every aspect of my life when I learned to let go. Eventually, what was shining on the inside was reflected on the outside. You revealed that it is okay to find a balance between being vulnerable and transparent, even with the pain I have experienced in my own life. You helped me change my perspective and find my own truth. Thank you for teaching me that love starts with me. I have always seen the good in people and loved others deeply, but you taught me how to love myself deeply.

I transformed into a version of myself that I never knew existed. It was your storm that reminded me that change and healing begin with me. I now honor the days I feel low but find the good in every day. I now honor endings, embrace new beginnings, and carry new wisdom moving forward.

Thank you.

Chapter 13

Who Am I Becoming?

I cannot say I truly know who I am yet because I believe the best version of myself is still a work in progress. My journey is still unfolding, and this time, the "rebirth" of the new me is coming to the horizon. Although, when I look in the mirror today, I see a strong woman who has faced some of the most difficult challenges in life at such a young age. The events I have been through and challenged with were supposed to break me. I could have easily stayed in my dark space and been angry with the world, but I made a choice. I decided to use my pain to better my life and continue to assist others in their journey.

I chose to help others with grief because it is a critical time in your life when you need at least one person to make a difference. I reached out to others who also lost their parents or just reached out to someone that was going through a traumatic event and needed some encouraging words even if I did not know what was going on. I was not looking for anything in return; I just wanted people to know it was okay and hoped that my experiences could give them what every person in this world looks for – **hope**.

I am using all my wisdom and knowledge that I have gained in the past five years to create a new foundation. I now show myself the same kindness, compassion, and love I show everyone else. As a 'new me' is emerging, I realize some of the things that used to make me happy no longer make me happy and that is okay. I enjoy simple things now, especially things that bring me peace. I think and respond differently, and most importantly, I find time to reflect. I still reflect on the things I went through because I am still processing everything that happened. Life can turn upside down with no warning, and you may not have been prepared for the storm.

Five years later, I am so proud of myself and my journey. I am in a better space than I used to be, and I know that I can handle any challenges that may be ahead. The person I am becoming is someone I was meant to be all along, but it took **many** challenges to get to this point.

I am by far nowhere near perfect, though. I still go through the emotions of grief on every level, but they are not as overwhelming as when my mother first passed away. My grief now is more related to shedding old aspects of myself. Before my mom passed away, I despised change. I liked the "routine" of everything and was content with how life was. Fast forward with time, I have grown to embrace change. I would not say I am fully in love with change just yet, but I have learned that change is the mirror image of growth, and I love growth.

Most people, including myself, have been afraid to take risks and face the unknown. However, I have learned that if you do not take risks, you may have regrets in your life at some point. Your life is full of possibilities, and the only person who can discover what is on the other side is you. This could also mean leaving your comfort zone of pain and trauma. This can be difficult because as human beings, we are supposed to evolve, and if we feel stagnant or afraid to become better, we must figure out what changes need to be applied.

Every new chapter in your life requires you to let go of something. It is not easy, but once you start to let go of your control and adjust to the new version of yourself, it will become more freeing. When you let go, you allow the things meant for you to come in— holding space for new people, experiences, and things that will assist with your ascent.

This takes a lot of patience and acceptance. I have learned that the grief process is a continuous thing in life. It just does not have to be a deep sorrow from just death. It can be grieving that life does not stay the same forever.

Who you are becoming will cost you changes in all aspects of your life, but as long as you continue to focus on the end outcome—healing and becoming a better you—you will reap every benefit and reward.

Chapter 14

Words of Wisdom

Where Am I Today?

It has been five years since my mom has passed away. I am currently in another transition in my life. I am building a new foundation within myself elevating away from my emotional wound. My goal moving forward is to see who I am **without** it. I am currently shedding this old layer of myself and walking into my new chapter. I am grieving this because I do not recognize the 'new me' that is being birthed. I have healed many aspects of myself which I am proud of, but I am changing the narrative and using my emotional wound to become my greatest strength. I am still a work in progress and still learning how to surrender and let go. However, I am excited to see where this new foundation and chapter takes me.

I have made peace with my mom physically not being here and all the wounds that have shaped me. I later realized this is what she would want for me. My mom wanted me to **heal from my past, be happy, and be at peace**. I will always miss my mom, but I know that she is watching over me. I have overcome so much, and I am proud to be where I am. I was able to pick up the pieces and **renew** the person that was once broken. With time, grace, and gaining wisdom, I was able to transform into a confident and resilient woman. I would not have believed you if you told me five years ago that I would be standing in this position today. I have made peace with my past, and I am hopeful for my future. I am currently making space for something bigger and better in my life. I am living in the present moment with a deeper understanding of life. I am also trying to learn to be more open, transparent, and allow myself to be seen through everything I have been through. I am creating a new foundation for my life. I am on a journey learning how to act out of **love** and not pain and trauma. I am enjoying every moment and following where my soul takes me.

In this current moment, I can say I am **happy**. I have everything I need and want, not even materialistically; I have the peace, wealth (calm mind), and happiness I worked so hard to obtain since my mom passed away. Every day is a new day for me to explore this new version of myself. Some days are challenging, and other days, I am at ease with my journey. The path ahead can be quite scary, but I have an inner knowing that everything will be okay.

Reflection

Life has so many twists and turns. We believe we control many things, but unexpected events come into our lives for a greater purpose.

Grief has been a true blessing for me. Grief taught me many things and it showed me where I held deep pain within myself. However, it also showed me that I was making space for better days ahead. It provided me many gifts such as strength, compassion, and deeper appreciation for my life. Most importantly, grief taught me how to love myself.

I would not trade my journey for anything. I am more aware of the little things than ever before, cherishing every hug and conversation, and creating memories every second. It was a huge turning point in my life and helped me ascend in all aspects of my life.

I accomplished many things in my life, but the greatest accomplishment was turning my pain into motivation to help others become the best versions of themselves. People have recognized my growth, and I think that was the most fulfilling reward over anything I have. Ultimately, everyone has free will and makes their own choices, but I try to **lead** my life by example. I am now trying to **empower** others to take their power back, love themselves, and grow.

It was my **darkness** that helped me find the **light** within. I ultimately learned that my light helped others during their darker days. I encourage those battling with anxiety, low self-esteem, depression, or any other mental illnesses/wounds to invest in healing themselves. Ask the higher source to guide you in the direction you need to take to accomplish this aspect in your life.

I also highly suggest seeking out healthy resources to cope with the grief process, especially in the beginning. The emotions can be very overwhelming, and you feel like they are running your life. Everyone handles situations differently but remember that you are not alone, and there is always someone there to listen. Please remember that the way you feel in the beginning will start to subside; however, there is no timeline of when that may occur. Only you know what resources you truly need to bring healing into your life. For me, I knew that I could no longer hold all these emotions in and dedicated myself to finding healthy resources to help me transform my emotions into something greater.

Reminders

Remember, grief is losing your loved one, a job, a relationship, a friendship, or any other event that you have loved in your life. It can be related to any area in your life that is changing, including yourself. Grief can be in every type of event, but I promise brighter days are always ahead.

Be patient throughout your journey, especially with yourself. This is not an overnight transformation, and some days may be harder than others. The key is to stay consistent and dedicated to your journey. Sometimes you may feel like you are going backward, but you truly are always moving forward. Be kind to yourself during this journey and know that you are doing the best you can. **Losing a loved one, whether someone who passed away or someone who is no longer in your life, is a traumatic experience. Please understand that while you may feel alone, you are not.** I used to think no one understood how I was feeling and that this journey was unfair. However, many people have been through this before or are going through it but do not express themselves. Take the time to process what you need to get through your journey. Those who love you will understand. Grief is a complex thing to understand and deal with.

Do not be discouraged if you are not where you want to be just yet. The other side of the tunnel may seem far away, but when you let go of timelines and expectations, you may be at the other side sooner than you think.

Sometimes, we want to get to the end outcome right away (not feeling pain), but I must say the healing journey has been a gift. Patience will bring in stillness, peace, and more happiness if you allow it. Remember putting the past behind you is challenging, including your trauma. Letting go is tough— something I am still learning and probably will continue to learn throughout my life. Be thankful for the delays, detours, and setbacks because they all serve a purpose in our lives. Accept things for what they were, what they are, and what they may be. Yesterday happened, tomorrow has not arrived, but today is the present moment, which you have complete control over. Remember that we all make mistakes, but they do not define who you are on a core level.

Learn to love others for where they are in their journey, including yourself. Do not hold resentment towards anyone. Acknowledge the loss, yes, but try to open your mind from another perspective. Ask yourself what traumas do you need to confront, how you can learn to break karmic cycles, and how you can continue to grow in life. Challenge your beliefs and thoughts.

Trust your process and let it unfold the way it is supposed to. Regardless of where you are in your life and any type of grief you come across, you can pour the love back into yourself and truly make an investment in yourself. Recognize your unhealthy patterns; this is a form of self-love. Strip away the distractions and disruptions in life because if you do not, grief may get your attention as it did mine.

Do not be resistant to your process. When you are resistant, it blocks you from what is truly meant for you. Remember, no one can heal, fix, or save you. Only you can do that. No one can stop the wounds from running your life except you. Love people and all your experiences for what they taught you, and love people for where they are in their journey. Everyone in your life is here to teach you something, whether it is to love yourself more, tell you to face your fears and pain, help you elevate to a higher love within yourself, or simply to just love you.

Look at each chapter of your life as an opportunity, even the painful ones. Our experiences, pain, and trials will always give us the answers we are truly looking for. This is where we can let go of the life we dreamt for ourselves and allow God to present us with the life that is truly meant for us. Be authentic, transparent, and open. It may be what someone else needs. We all have gifts and talents that are meant to be shared. Turn your **pain** into **wisdom** to move forward in a better direction.

Where to Start?

Start small. The beginning is not easy, especially when you do not have a set guideline on where to start but investing love back into yourself is a great place to begin.

Remember, you are much stronger than you think. While no one could ever replace your loss and the love for that person, they are shining down on you, encouraging you to keep going. The path ahead may be scary, challenging, and frustrating at times, but you will grow and expand just as I hope I am helping you expand with this book. Each day is a new day to find positivity and purpose while reflecting on memories of the person you lost in your life. You carry your loved one's strength and love with you every day, even if you are unaware of it at first. I have overcome so many obstacles on my journey because I reflected on how my mom overcame obstacles in her final days. You are a **warrior** and can overcome the most uncomfortable emotions, including grief.

I encourage you to continue to push forward, no matter how difficult the loss may be. Take things one day at a time, know that tomorrow always brings the possibility of a brighter day, and remember you are not alone. **Keep going even when you feel weak, discouraged, or uninspired because that is where your character develops.** You may need to take time off from work or go somewhere peaceful to renew. Allow yourself to slow down and go within.

Final Words

Some days, I thought it was impossible and believed how I felt (in the beginning) would never end, but looking back, I realize I have come so far, even more than I probably can comprehend. Love is the most powerful emotion in the universe and continues to expand every day. Without love, we cannot grieve, and most importantly, we cannot grow. **Remember you are love.** I think grief has brought deep reflection in myself in understanding what true love is. **True love starts with yourself.**

We all have a story. We all have gone through some sort of trauma or loss in our lives, but it should not keep us held hostage from a better future.

You will persevere through all challenges and transform into a phoenix.

You are in control of your destiny and fate. Pain and

trauma become a part of our identity, and we decide to either use them as a tool to better our lives or let them control our lives.

Self-love is the key ingredient of setting yourself free from your pain.

However, one thing I question is when we heal, who are we when we no longer operate from our pain and trauma? This is where your true power lies.

I wish you much love, hope, and peace along your journey.

"I Am"

As I was writing this book, I felt inspired to share "I Am" and "I Believe" affirmations with you. You can say these affirmations as many times throughout the day and add more to your list. I hope they make a difference in your life.

- I Am Strong.

- I Believe in New Beginnings.

- I Am Powerful.

- I Believe that My Future is Bright.

- I am Loving.

- I Believe I am Growing.

- I am Kind.

- I Believe in Healing.

- I am Smart.

- I Believe in Transformations.

- I am Confident.

- I Believe in Myself.

- I am Bigger than My Grief.

- I Believe in Overcoming Obstacles.

- I am Worthy.

- I Believe I am Worthy.

- I am Deserving.

- I Believe Grief Gives Me Room for Growth.

- I am Whole.

- I Believe in Miracles.

- I am More Than Enough.

- I Believe My Future is Bigger than My Past.

- I am a Special Person.

- I Believe in My Dreams and Goals.

- I am Positive.

- I Believe in My Higher Self.

- I am Thankful for New Beginnings.

- I Believe in Inspiring Others.

- I am a Warrior.

- I Believe in Reflecting.

- I am Safe.

- I Believe in Growth.

- I am Secure.

- I Believe in Self-Love.

- I am Thankful to Help Others.

- I Believe in New Opportunities.

- I am One with God.

- I Believe I am Shedding Old Layers of Myself.

- I am Becoming a Better Version of Myself.

- I Believe in Inner Peace.

- I am Compassionate.

- I Believe Every Moment is an Opportunity.

- I am Love.

- I Believe I Can Change.

- I am Facing "Old" and "Outdated" Sides of Myself to Make More Room for More Light.

- I Believe I Can Create the Life I Desire for Myself.

- I am Thankful for My Journey.

- I Believe There is a Higher Purpose for Me.

- I am Healing.

- I Believe I Have a Story to Share.

- I am Patient.

- I Believe in Guiding Others.

- I am Divine.

- I Believe I am the Light.

- I am Letting Go of What No Longer Serves Me.

- I Believe in My Destiny.

- I am Learning to Love Myself Unconditionally.

- I Believe in Acceptance.

- I am a Leader.

- I am Proud of Myself.

- I Believe I am More Than Enough.

- I am Loved.

- I Believe in Breaking Old Cycles.

- I am Learning to Be Gentle with Myself.

- I Believe in Creating Healthy Habits for Myself.

- I am Assertive When I Have to Be.

- I Believe in my Future.

- I am Overcoming My Past.

"A Journey Back to Love"

By Caitlin Burr

I've cried and cried because I'm searching for
something that I have not found. It's a piece of me,
but it feels like it's out of town.

I traveled far and long trying to come back home,
but this journey has left me all alone. I have all but
one piece. Where can I find it to make me complete?

A quiet whisper told me to look inside. My heart is
full and feels alive. I am finally free and able to fly
like a dove.

Love is me and I am love. I'm no longer searching
because I'm the missing piece. My journey back
home is already complete.

About the Author

Caitlin Burr is a young writer who wants to share her experiences and wisdom with the world in hopes to enlighten and empower others in their journey of healing from grief. Caitlin earned a B.S. in Criminal Justice and Political Science from Frostburg State University. She also earned an M.S. in Homeland Security from Towson University. Caitlin hopes to start a charity and healing center for those who have gone through traumatic experiences in their lives to show that it is possible to heal and move forward. She currently resides in Maryland.

Caitlin would love to connect with her readers beyond this book. She has created an author's website for her readers to contact her with their thoughts and questions about the healing journey.

www.passionloveandpurpose.com

You can also follow her on Instagram at
passion.love.purpose

She looks forward to connecting with you!

Acknowledgments

Thank you, Phoenix Blue Academic Editing Services, for the opportunity to work with Dr. Tiffanie James Parker. Thank you for your hard work to enhance the content of this book. You are a phenomenal editor!

I would like to thank Dorothea Taylor for creating this book cover. Grief, Growth, and Gratitude: A Journey Back to Love would not be the same without your design. Thank you for your time, dedication, and energy on this project. You are beyond talented.

Thank you to my family and friends for your continuous support. I am thankful for your encouragement throughout my life. I love you all!